TRAVELLERS

KERALA &
SOUTHERN
INDIA

By
ANIL MULCHANDANI

Written by Anil Mulchandani, updated by Debbie Stowe
Original photography by CPA Media

Published by Thomas Cook Publishing
A division of Thomas Cook Tour Operations Limited.
Company registration no. 1450464 England
The Thomas Cook Business Park, Unit 9, Coningsby Road,
Peterborough PE3 8SB, United Kingdom
E-mail: books@thomascook.com, Tel: + 44 (0) 1733 416477
www.thomascookpublishing.com

Produced by Cambridge Publishing Management Limited
Burr Elm Court, Main Street, Caldecote CB23 7NU

ISBN: 978-1-84157-995-5

First edition © 2006 Thomas Cook Publishing
This second edition © 2008
Text © Thomas Cook Publishing
Maps © Thomas Cook Publishing
Transport map © Communicarta Limited

Series Editor: Maisie Fitzpatrick
Production/DTP: Steven Collins

Printed and bound in Italy by Printer Trento

Cover photography: Front L-R: © Ripani Massimo/4-CR;
© Robert Leon/Alamy; © Larry Williams/Masterfile
Back L-R: © Helene Rogers/Alamy; © Ripani Massimo/4-CR

The paper used for this book has been independently certified as having
been sourced from well-managed forests and recycled wood or fibre
according to the rules of the Forest Stewardship Council.
This book has been printed and bound in Italy by Printer Trento S.r.l.,
an FSC certified company for printing books on FSC mixed paper in
compliance with the chain of custody and on products labelling standards.

FSC
Mixed Sources
Product group from well-managed
forests and recycled wood or fibre
Cert no. CQ-COC-000012
www.fsc.org
© 1996 Forest Stewardship Council

Contents

KEY TO MAPS

⭐ Start of walk/tour   🏛 Museum

ℹ️ Information   ⌁ Railway

✝ Church   ▲ Mountain

Introduction

Kerala runs along the Arabian Sea coastline of southwestern India, rising eastward from the sea to the forested peaks of the Western Ghats, with intermediate fertile midlands producing the spices that attracted Chinese, Arab, Jewish and European traders to the harbours of Kozhikode and Kochi. Justly famous for its beaches and lush green backwaters, Kerala is among the most popular destinations in India.

Isolated for centuries from the rest of India by its natural boundaries of hills and the sea, Kerala has cities and towns with colourful temples, European-style churches, and mosques that mirror the distinctive local cultures and international influences from centuries of global maritime contact. The traders, settlers and invaders brought with them their religions, and so a healthy Christian and Muslim population balances the Hindu majority of Kerala.

While agriculture remains the mainstay of the economy, the state government and local enterprise have recognised the importance of tourism as a revenue earner and have developed a sophisticated infrastructure that presents the scenic and cultural charms of Kerala in the comfort of luxurious hotels and resorts, houseboats, restored heritage houses and plantation bungalows.

The neighbouring state of Tamil Nadu, like Kerala, has an attractive coastline with beaches, palm groves and paddy fields, and green hills rich in wildlife and spice plantations, but its appeal lies in its remarkable devotional architecture from the shore temples of Mahabalipuram and Rameshwaram to the bustling temple towns of Kanchipuram, Thanjavur and Madurai. In contrast, the former French enclave of Pondicherry has a distinctly European feel, with its churches, colonial buildings, and restaurants serving French food and wine.

Karnataka ranges scenically from some of the wettest sections of the Western Ghats near its west coast, draped in dense deciduous forests known for their wildlife, coffee estates, waterfalls and the source of great rivers like the Krishna, Kaveri and Tungabhadra, to the historic towns of the interior, surrounded by ancient granite and barren rocks. A succession of dynasties has used the rocks of Karnataka to create some of India's finest architectural gems, such as the superbly carved temples of Halebid, Belur, Hampi, Badami and Pattadakal, the majestic mosques of Bijapur and Bidar, and the grand palaces of Mysore, which was once the seat of power of the princely state that comprised much of today's Karnataka before India's independence in 1947. The capital of Karnataka today is Bangalore, the modern face of Southern India and one of the world's largest centres of information technology (IT) and software development. Bangalore is also known for its fashion garment exports.

Like Bangalore, Hyderabad, which is the capital of Andhra Pradesh, has evolved into an IT and outsourcing hub.

Once the capital of India's largest princely state, Hyderabad has impressive palaces and museums, and forts that protected the state from invasions. A few hours' drive east from Hyderabad is Nagarjunakonda, the most substantial remains of Buddhist civilisation in Southern India. The heartland of Telugu arts, crafts and culture lies further east in the fertile Krishna and Godavari deltas, whose attractions include a number of ancient sites and a living tradition of weaving which has been nurtured by the cotton production of the region.

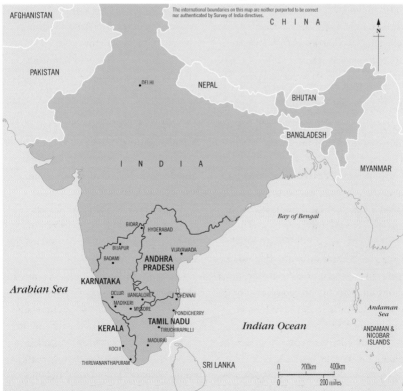

The land

Southern India entices travellers with a variety of beautiful scenery, from fine beaches along the Arabian Sea and Bay of Bengal to hill stations like Kodaikanal, Ooty and Munnar near Anamudi Peak, which at more than 2,695m (8,842ft) is the highest mountain in Southern India. According to local legend, Kerala was created by Parsurama, an incarnation of Lord Vishnu, whom the gods promised as much land as he could reclaim with a hurl of an axe.

Geography

This creation myth may have its origins in geographical reality, for the coastal areas of Kerala were raised from the sea by geological forces, and the landscape has continued to evolve ever since with silt deposited by the rivers and tides. The backwaters (*see pp40–41*) are a distinctive feature of Kerala's coastal geography.

Running parallel to the coast towards the southern tip of the peninsula, the Western Ghats are richly vegetated with evergreen and deciduous forests, including some of India's most substantial tracts of rainforest and important wildlife reserves.

Great rivers such as the Kaveri, the Krishna and the Godavari rise in the Western Ghats and flow eastward to drain into the Bay of Bengal, while the relatively shorter westward-flowing rivers create beautiful scenery including huge waterfalls, dense forests and large lakes in Kerala and Karnataka.

The Deccan Plateau lies between the Western Ghats and the Eastern Ghats, a less dramatic chain comprising massive blocks of hills less than 1,500m (5,000ft) high in interrupted stretches through Andhra and Tamil Nadu. Consisting of some of the world's oldest rocks and layers of lava from ancient volcanic eruptions, the Deccan is veined by rivers such as the Tungabhadra and Krishna that gave rise to the great empires of Andhra and Karnataka. Beyond the slopes of the plateau, the east coast is an affluent area, with the ports of Chennai and Visakhapatnam, and fertile deltas. The southeast coast has significant mangrove forests that are nurseries for marine life, as well as being important areas for birdlife.

Economy

The most significant development in the economy of Southern India in the last 20 years has been the IT boom. As well as Indian software companies, multinationals attracted by the qualified yet relatively inexpensive technical expertise of the four states where English is widely spoken, have invested in software development companies in Bangalore, Hyderabad, Chennai and other cities.

The engineering industries of Tamil Nadu, Karnataka and Andhra have also seen a boom with the growing demand for aircraft, cars, railway rolling stock and machinery in India's rising economy. Other important industrial sectors are leather-tanning in Chennai, textile mills in Coimbatore, hosiery at Tirupur, chemicals and fertilisers, sugar mills, mining, and the small-scale industries of Sivakasi and Hosur.

While the IT boom has been an urban phenomenon, the bedrock of the local economy is agriculture, with Kerala growing much of India's rubber, spices, lemongrass, coconuts, tapioca and cocoa. Tea and coffee plantations thrive in the Western Ghats, while the river plains, deltas and coastal areas produce rice, sugar cane, groundnuts and other oilseeds, and cotton. Fishing is another important revenue source.

The tea plantation at Munnar

History

10th–5th centuries BC	Megalithic sites show that a sophisticated civilisation has existed in Kerala for centuries.
3rd century BC	The Cheras, Cholas and Pandyas rule Southern India.
1st century AD	Thomas the Apostle is believed to have visited Kerala in AD 52 and introduced Christianity. Jews land at Muziris in about AD 70.
2nd and 3rd centuries	The Buddhist architecture of the Satavahana rulers of Andhra reaches its apogee. Tamil Sangam literature, which flourished in the early Christian era, offers an insight into socioeconomics and culture in Kerala under the Chera kings.
6th and 7th centuries	Malik Ibn Dinar, a disciple of Muhammad, brings Islam to Kerala, and establishes one of the first mosques in India in the 7th century AD. The Chalukya dynasties thrive in Karnataka.
7th century	The Pallava ruler Narasimhavarman makes Mahabalipuram (Mamallapuram) famous as a port.
9th century	A new Chera dynasty emerges. *Perumal*, or ruler, was the sovereign power, but people's rights were acknowledged by the presence of elected representatives. Malayalam emerges as a distinct language.
10th and 11th centuries	The Chola rulers of the neighbouring Tamil Coromandel coast bring an end to Chera sovereignty in 1102.
13th–15th centuries	The Islamic conquerors of Northern India make incursions into Southern India. Vijayanagar rulers respond by amalgamating into a kingdom at Hampi.
1498–1502	Vasco da Gama makes landfall near Calicut.
16th century	The Deccan Sultanates dominate Karnataka and great monuments are built at Bidar and Bijapur.

17th century	Mughal Aurangzeb extends his empire into Southern India. The Marathas extend their rule to Central Tamil Nadu.
1604	A Dutch alliance with the Zamorin begins a joint effort to displace the Portuguese in Kerala.
1653	Syrian Christians revolt against the Portuguese attempts to Latinise the church, a turning point in the Syrian Christian history.
1663	The Dutch succeed in displacing the Portuguese from Kochi, Cranganore, Kollam, Allepey and Cannonore.
1761–99	The Sultans of Mysore dominate Karnataka and make incursions into Kerala.
1795	The British seize the Dutch fort at Kochi.
1800	The British subjugate Kerala and divide it into the British province of Malabar, and the princely states of Kochi and Travancore.
1805	After a five-year struggle against the British, Pazhassi Raja dies in battle and is given a hero's funeral.
1812	Forces are called in to crush the tribal revolt against collecting taxes in cash instead of in kind.
1836–56	Tensions between the Hindu landlords and Muslim tenants result in the Mappilla Riots.
1885	The Indian National Congress is formed and instigates talks with the British.
1919	Kerala's committee of the National Congress is convened at Trichur.
1947	India gains independence and Kerala becomes part of Madras State.
1956	Southern India is reorganised into the states of Tamil Nadu, Andhra Pradesh, Kerala and Mysore (later renamed Karnataka).
1957–2008	For more on recent political developments, *see p11.*

Politics

As a country of considerable religious diversity, India has sustained a constitutional democratic system for nearly 60 years in the face of tremendous pressure and challenges, with the possible exception of two years (1975–7) when Indira Gandhi, as prime minister, imposed a state of emergency banning political activity. Key features of the constitution are secularism, equal rights for women, universal suffrage, human rights and a ban on untouchability.

India's government

India is a sovereign democratic republic, and every citizen 18 years of age or over is eligible to vote. The president is the official head but exercises his powers under the authority of the prime minister and his council.

The *Lok Sabha* (Council of People) consists of 552 members, with 530 members representing the 28 states, up to 20 members representing the Union Territories, and two members of the Anglo-Indian Community to be nominated by the president, if the community is not already adequately represented in the House. The upper house, *Rajya Sabha* (Council of States), has 12 members nominated by the president and 233 members elected by the state assemblies.

The 29 states have legislative assemblies with the governor as the official head nominated by the president, and the chief minister and his cabinet responsible for the actual administration of the state. Like the central government, most of the states have two houses of parliament – the *Rajya Sabha*, comprising mainly nominated members, and the *Vidhan Sabha*, consisting of elected members.

The central government controls the armed forces, aviation, railways, postal services, currency and international affairs. The state governments are responsible for industry, agriculture, roads, forestry and environment, and internal security.

The political scene in India

Congress Party leader Jawaharlal Nehru became the first prime minister of India in 1947, and Congress has won the majority of the general elections held in the country. At the 11th general elections, in 1996, Congress was defeated by the Bharatiya Janta Party (BJP). A coalition called the United Front was formed, but it fell in 1998 when the Congress Party withdrew its support, and the BJP came to power with Atal Behari Vajpayee as the prime minister. The BJP and Vajpayee also won the 1999 elections, forming a coalition government.

With an unprecedented boom in the economy, BJP launched the 'India Shining' campaign which focused on their achievements in increased exports, technological progress, image building, tourism and IT, but this was effectively countered by the Congress Party which appealed to the rural masses and won the 2004 elections, with Dr Manmohan Singh becoming prime minister. The next elections are scheduled for 2009.

Politics in Southern India

Regional political parties have been strong forces in the elections of Southern India. Tamil Nadu's elections have been dominated alternately by the DMK from 1967, when it defeated the Congress Party, and AIADMK, which split from the main DMK body in 1972. During the 2006 elections, DMK was elected to power with its head, M Karunanidhi, as chief minister, beating the AIADMK whose chief, J Jayalalitha, had a long spell as chief minister of Tamil Nadu.

In Andhra, Telugu Desam, formed by N T Rama Rao, dominated the elections in the 1980s. After the Congress Party came to power in 1989, Telugu Desam was elected back to power in 1994, and N Chandrababu Naidu, who succeeded NT Rama Rao, brought in a technological revolution, making Hyderabad one of the software capitals of India. However, in the 2004 elections

he was outvoted by the Congress Party who swept back to power, with Y S Rajashekhara Reddy sworn in as chief minister. The party has since gone on to win several more local elections.

Kerala is unique in having democratically elected the Communist Party of India in 1957, when the first legislative assembly was formed for the state. The recent elections have been dominated by the Left Democratic Front, led by the Communist Party of India. Since 2006 it has had a majority of 56 seats out of a total of 140.

Karnataka's politics have been largely dominated by the Congress Party, but in 2006 the JD(S)-BJP coalition was elected into power. B S Yeddyurappa was appointed chief minister in November 2007.

Government Museum, Chennai

Culture

Despite its long history of global maritime contact and European colonisation, Kerala has retained its distinctive cultural identity. For many visitors to Kerala, its tolerant culture, embracing Hinduism, Judaism, Christianity and Islam, is a particular attraction, and this is reflected in the state's dance and drama, as well as in the martial arts and alternative medicine.

The caste system

Brahmins are at the apex of the Hindu caste system, which is a system of inherited social groupings within the society. Traditionally Brahmins have been priests and learned people, but today they are seen in various professions, although they generally follow rules of conduct such as strict vegetarianism.

The Nairs have been a dominant force in the political and social life of Kerala for a long time. They followed a matrilineal system of inheritance that many believe has its origins in the 10th and 11th centuries when Nair warriors went to battle against the Cholas. This practice became illegal in 1956 when the Hindu Succession Act gave equal rights of inheritance to men and women.

Traditionally, Nairs lived in community homes called *Tharawads*, which were designed to house the extended family. Women lived with their brothers and sisters, and their children, with shared kitchens and dining areas. Between 50 and 80 people often shared a large courtyard house called a *Nalakettu*.

Usually landowners, Nairs are credited with the preservation of the Kallaripayattu martial arts and the Kathakali dance drama. The Nairs continue to influence politics and have formed the Nair Service Society to promote their aims and aspirations.

With such good literacy and political awareness, there has been a tremendous backlash against the caste system in parts of India, especially concerning untouchability, and the domination of the upper castes has declined.

Tribes and nomadic groups

With Southern India's high literacy rate, many tribes have seen improved standards of living, but some tribal villages still subsist on marginal agriculture and on gathering forest produce such as honey, and they have retained their traditional lifestyles. The main tribal groups – travellers of the Malayarayan, Mannan, Muthuvan, Oorali, Paliyan, Hill Pulayan, Malapandaram, Ulladan, Malayan, Paniya and Adiya – are likely to meet near tourist destinations, especially in the Idukki and Wayanad Districts. Todas near Ooty (see pp138–9) in Tamil Nadu live in igloo-like bamboo and grass huts and wear brightly patterned shawls. Other tribal groups include the Kotas, who have a musical tradition; the Kurumbas, who have mostly taken employment at plantations; and the Irulas, known for their snake-catching skills. The Lambanis and other groups of Banjaras are semi-nomadic groups that are known for their embroidery skills in Andhra and Karnataka. Andhra has a number of tribal groups, most of them concentrated in the hills around Araku (see p141).

Language

The four principal languages of Southern India are Malayalam spoken in Kerala, Tamil in Tamil Nadu, Kannada in Karnataka and Telugu in Andhra Pradesh. All of these have Dravidian roots with some Sanskrit influences. Konkani is spoken along the coast of Karnataka. Dakhani and Urdu, languages that developed from an amalgamation of Indian languages and those of Islamic invaders such as Arabic, Persian and Turkish, are widely spoken in Hyderabad and some other historic cities of Andhra and Karnataka. French is still spoken by some of the residents of Pondicherry (see pp112–13), which is now a Union Territory. English is widely spoken in Southern India, especially in the cities of Chennai, Bangalore, Hyderabad, Kochi and Thiruvananthapuram.

Lambani tribal costume

Music and dance
See pp58–9.

Religion

Southern India has a Hindu majority. In Kerala, about a fifth of the population follows Christianity and a quarter Islam. Andhra Pradesh has a significant Muslim population in and around its capital, Hyderabad.

Hinduism

Hinduism is a religious tradition with ancient roots dating back to the third and second millennia BC. With no founder, prophet or church-like organisation to define the rules, Hinduism has embraced new features and a diversity of religious beliefs even up until recent times. The holy books of the Hindus are the *Vedas* (incorporating the *Upanishads* as the final volumes), which are often considered the foundation of Indian philosophy, with epics like the *Ramayana* and *Mahabharata*, and the *Bhagavadgita* which is based on the philosophies of Lord Krishna as they were related to warrior prince Arjun in an episode of the *Mahabharata*.

Hindus believe in a cycle of reincarnation determined by their *karma*, the consequences of former actions that can flow into the next life. The aims of a Hindu are to attain material wealth honestly (*artha*), satisfy all desires (*kama*) and perform all duties (*dharma*), all of which will lead, through good *karma*, to *moksha*, liberation from the endless rebirth cycle.

An aspect of Hinduism that most visitors to India find hard to understand is the multitude of gods and goddesses. Actually, most of them are incarnations and manifestations of a few, and this may be the result of Hinduism incorporating regional beliefs into its pantheon. Three Gods are considered integral to Hinduism: Brahma as the creator, Vishnu as the preserver of the universe (usually worshipped as one of his many incarnations that rids the world of destroying forces like demons) and Shiva, the destroyer, who is worshipped in many forms, such as Natraja when he dances to destroy evil. The consort of Brahma is Sarasvati, the goddess of learning. Vishnu's consort Lakshmi is worshipped as the goddess of wealth, and Shiva's consort Parvati has many manifestations, including Durga and Kali, goddesses of power and destruction. Most Hindus start a new venture by worshipping Ganesh, the elephant-headed son of Lord Shiva, who is said to bring luck, knowledge and prosperity.

Some key features of Hindu religious traditions are *darshan* (visions), which denote the importance of visiting holy places, *puja* or ritualistic worship, and cremation of the dead.

From the 8th century, the *Bhakti* tradition or devotional form of Hinduism emerged in Southern India and became popular in the rest of the country as well. This was a period of resurgence for Hinduism, as Buddhism and Jainism were becoming dominant in Southern India, and saw poet saints converting kingdoms such as Madurai from Jainism to Hinduism. Some of the songs of the Tamil poet saints are still sung. Leaders such as Sankaracharya brought in a resurgence of Hinduism in Kerala.

Christianity

It is widely believed by the Christians of Kerala that one of Christ's Apostles, St Thomas, settled in Malabar in AD 52 and introduced Christianity to Kerala. In AD 345, a Christian Syrian merchant named Thomas landed on the Kerala coast and preached Christianity based on the practices of the Syrian Church. In the 9th century a number of Christians from Syria settled in Kerala, and this led to the Christians of Kerala calling themselves Syrian Christians.

The Portuguese promoted Roman Catholic practices, but the Syrian Christians resented the Latinisation of their Church and took the Oath of the Coonan Cross separating their Church from Rome. In 1662, however, many of the Syrian churches reunited with Rome.

The Dutch were not very tolerant of the Portuguese Roman Catholic

Christian Sisters serve the local community

churches and they converted churches, like that of St Francis in Kochi, into their own Protestant ones. The British introduced the Anglican Church, and among its members were the Syrian Jacobite Group.

The most important pilgrimage for most Christians in Southern India is to Our Lady of Health, Vailankani; the shrine was established in Tamil Nadu in the 17th century following a series of miracles and apparitions. It attracts a large crowd of worshippers, including non-Christians.

Islam

Islam began in Mecca around the 7th century, when the Prophet Mohammad compiled revelations from Allah, and was brought to Kerala in the same century by one of the Prophet's followers, Malik Ibn Dinar.

However, the history of Islam in Southern India is generally attributed to trade with the Middle East. The religion found a tolerant society, and the support of Hindu princes, like the Zamorins of Calicut, helped Islam grow in Kerala. Islamic contact grew as the Arabs gained a monopoly over trade between the Zamorin-dominated Malabar Coast and the Mediterranean.

To be a Muslim is to accept the fact that there is no god but Allah, and Mohammad is his prophet. This simple principle of Islam, submission to god, is called *shahada* and is the bedrock of the belief. By uttering these words, a Muslim commits to a life of praise-giving obedience to god. The *Quran* is the holy book of the Muslims and the supreme authority on the Islamic faith. The five pillars of Islam are the profession of faith regarding the one God and Mohammed as God's messenger, worship five times daily, almsgiving, fasting in the month of *Ramadhan*, and the pilgrimage to Mecca. Alcohol and pork are prohibited and meat must be prepared in a way called *halal* that involves draining the blood of an animal while it is alive. Gambling and charging interest on loans are forbidden.

Judaism

There are ancient accounts of Jewish contacts with Kerala. Some refer back to trade with King Solomon, and escaping injustice in Assyria, fleeing slavery in Babylon or the destruction of Jerusalem. Referred to as 'Black Jews', they were later supplemented by the 'White Jews' fleeing the Inquisitions of Spain and Portugal in the 16th century, and later by Ashkenazi Jews escaping the pogroms. The Jews were influential merchants, and in the 10th and 11th centuries a Jewish merchant, Joseph Rabban, was granted royal privileges by Raja Bhaskara Varma. The Raja of Kochi gave similar grants when Jews moved to Kochi after the near-destruction of the community by the Arabs in Malabar, and Portuguese persecution. Today, only a few Jewish families remain in Kochi after the mass migration to Israel in the 1950s.

Religion

Buddhism

Buddhism is based on the beliefs of
Sidhartha Gautama Buddha who was
born into a princely family in the 6th
century BC. His preaching is often
regarded as a reaction to Hinduism,
accepting the doctrine of reincarnation
and the law of *karma*, but rejecting the
concept of a pantheon of gods and the
caste system.

Once popular in Southern India,
Buddhism declined after the *Bhakti*
movement of Hinduism in the 8th
century. Some of the most significant
relics can be seen in Andhra Pradesh.
Tibetan settlements in Karnataka, most
of them in Kodagu district (*see pp94–5*),
have established Buddhist monasteries
near Bylakuppe including Namdroling,
known as the Golden Temple.

Jainism

Jainism is based on the teachings of
Mahavira, one of the 24 *tirthankaras*
(ford-makers) sacred to Jains. The key
features of the Jain religion are
liberation from the wheel of rebirth
and the belief that all life is sacred.
Strict vegetarianism is a feature of
Jainism, for Jains believe that even the
smallest life form has a soul.

There is now only a small Jain
population in Southern India,
including migrants from Rajasthan and
Gujarat, but there are historic Jain
temples and monastic caves in
Karnataka and Kerala, as well as living
temples in most cities. An important
pilgrimage for Jains is to
Sravanabelagola (*see pp92–3*) with its
colossal statue.

Gomateshvara statue, Sravanabelagola

Festivals

Besides the many religious festivals, there are exciting secular festivals, such as the boat races on the backwaters. Tourist offices can provide details of these as well as various cultural festivals at a number of tourist destinations, including Kochi, Thiruvananthapuram, Alappuzha, Kollam and Kovalam.

Pongal

14 January

Pongal is a Tamil harvest festival, coinciding with Makar Sankranti which is celebrated in the rest of India. Cows are decorated and processions can be seen on the streets of the state during the festival, and floor paintings are created outside many houses.

Sabarimala Festival

January

This is one of Kerala's most important festivals honouring Ayyappan, whom devotees believe to be born from the union of Shiva and Vishnu's female form Mohini. Dressed in black, devotees make the pilgrimage to Sabarimala with stops for ceremonies along the way. Ascending the 18 steps to the temple, they promise to bring an end to sin.

Thaipuram or Thai Pussam

January–February

This festival honours Subramaya or Kartikeyan, the God of War, at his temples in Kerala. This god has six heads denoting the five senses and the mind, and is depicted on a peacock.

Mannanam Convention

February

From 1894, this convention has been held in honour of Father Chavara, who is buried here and who is considered to be a saint because of his work with the lower classes. Since then, it has grown to become one of Asia's largest Christian Conventions.

Krishna Festival at Guruvayoor

February–March

This ten-day festival is celebrated with processions of elephants. The Krishna image is carried on top of an elephant during the last day's procession before it is bathed in the temple tank. Ritual bathing is a feature of the festival, as devotees want to share the water with the deity.

Shivratri

February–March

Maha Shivratri commemorates the night when Shiva danced the *Tandava*, dance of destruction, and is celebrated with feasting, fairs and devotional rituals. Fairs take place at Alwaye and Attappady.

Thiruvananthapuram Arat Festival

March–April

This is a ten-night festival at the Padmanabhaswamy Temple in Thiruvananthapuram, culminating in a procession which carries the idol on an elephant to the sea for ritual bathing.

Pooram

April–May

This festival is a magnificent spectacle at Thrissur, with elephants, decorated with gold, carrying beautiful parasols, and paraded to the accompaniment of drumming and firework displays.

Onam

August–September

The most important festival in Kerala, Onam celebrates the harvest and the reign of philanthropic King Mahabali. The celebrations are spectacular at Alappuzha, where boat races take place, and at Thrissur, where you can enjoy the elephant processions.

Chandankkudham Mahotsava

October

This festival is celebrated with sword play, singing, dancing, processions, elephant parades and fireworks at Beemapalli near Thiruvananthapuram. Muslims carry incense sticks to the tomb of Bheema Beevi, a woman pilgrim who travelled to Mecca and was said to have divine powers.

Other festivals include: the Malayalam Drama Festival at Kottayam (January), the Musical Festival at Thiruvananthapuram (January and February), the Nishagandhi Dance Festival (February), the food festival at Thiruvananthapuram (April), the Hampi Festival (November), the Kerala Kalamandalam Festival at Cheruthuruthy (December and January) and the Ashtamudi Craft and Art Festival at Kollam (December and January).

Colourful decorations for Pongal

Impressions

Southern India, covering the states of Kerala, Karnataka, Tamil Nadu and Andhra Pradesh, plus the Union Territory of Pondicherry, is a vast area. You will find varied and beautiful scenery, architectural gems including some of India's greatest temples, forts and palaces, wildlife reserves and traditions of fine arts, music, dance, handicrafts, literature and Ayurvedic medicine.

Architecture

While most studies of Southern India's architecture focus on the religious monuments, there are also excellent examples of domestic architecture, such as the mansions of the Chettiars of Tamil Nadu (*see p117*) that tourists can now visit, and the Nair houses of Kerala. Great forts were built at Golconda near Hyderabad, with systematic water storage and canal systems to withstand a siege.

The prosperity of the Nizam of Hyderabad and the Maharaja of Mysore, the two most affluent princely states in all of India, also saw great palaces built in Mysore (*see pp88–9*) and Hyderabad (*see pp120–21*). These palaces blended Hindu, Islamic and European styles of architecture in the late 19th and early 20th centuries, at a time when peace treaties between the British and the princes ushered in a period of flamboyance.

The European powers dominated Southern India from the 17th century,

and relics of colonial rule include the French buildings of Pondicherry town on the Tamil coast, Yanam town near the Andhra coast and Mahe on the Kerala coast. Dutch and Portuguese influences can be seen in the buildings of Kerala, while the British influence is evident in the impressive buildings of Chennai and Bangalore, as well as the colonial bungalows at hill stations such as Ooty and Munnar.

It is, however, the rich heritage of religious architecture that draws many travellers to Southern India.

Buddhist *stupas* of Andhra

Stupas are hemispherical structures that evolved from simple burial mounds into elaborate monuments. They usually consist of a carved gateway called a *torana*, railings around an enclosure and platforms called *vedica*, carved pillars, *chattrayashti*, which is a parasol or canopy, and an ambulatory. The ambulatory is for the ritual of *pradakshina*, or clockwise circumambulation, transporting the worshipper into a magical force field of divine realms. The hemispherical dome represents the sacred hill or axis linking heaven with earth, while the square platform, conical spire, crescent moon and circular disc represent cosmic

Sri Meenakshi, Madurai

elements that have symbolic significance. The Satavahana rulers built intricate *stupas* in Andhra Pradesh that can be seen at Nagarjunakonda (*see pp126–7*) and Amravati (*see p128*).

Temples

The Hindu temple design works on principles laid down by priests in manuals called *Shastras* that set out in detail everything from the building process to the layout and the symbolic significance of the elevations. The temple focuses on the sanctum as the home of the presiding deity, with a succession of halls or buildings leading to it for the worshippers to assemble in or move through for *darshan* (beholding) of the deity. Hindu architecture uses beams and columns for support. The Dravida temple architecture (*pp100–101*) evolved from the 6th century to the 17th century in Tamil Nadu and has distinctive features such as the *gopurams* or towering gates and pyramidal towering roofs. The Hoysala dynasty's temples in Karnataka have their own distinctive style of a star-shaped plinth with an ambulatory around the temple, and the hall inside has beautifully carved columns.

Mosques

The mosques and mausoleum complexes of northern Karnataka and western Andhra Pradesh are in the Indo-Islamic style, inspired by the Turkish and other Middle-Eastern roots of the Islamic rulers, but incorporating elements of the artistry of the Hindu craftsmen.

Culture shock

Despite a high literacy rate and quality of life by Indian standards, Kerala has a number of shocks for first-time visitors, such as crowds, poverty, dust, dirt and disease. Although most people in Kerala are used to tourists, do not be surprised if visitors from other states or residents of out-of-the-way places stare, crowd around, giggle and involve you in inane conversation out of curiosity. It is perfectly common in India to discuss personal matters, politics and religion, and you will often be asked about your family and income.

Bureaucratic hurdles, slow service, crowded roads and long queues can try your patience, as elsewhere in India.

Conduct

Body language

The most common greeting in India is palms joined together as in prayer, accompanied by a *namaste* (reverential bow). Shaking hands is becoming a common form of greeting in India, but only the most westernised Indians will shake hands with a woman. The right hand is used for eating, receiving and giving.

Religious etiquette

Despite an amazing religious and cultural diversity, etiquette is similar for most religious places in Kerala. You will have to take off your shoes to visit temples, mosques and churches, while smoking and shows of affection are considered disrespectful at all religious places. You should also dress modestly and not talk loudly in temples and mosques. Touching idols at temples may be prohibited. Some Hindu temples in Kerala, especially those in the southern districts, do not allow foreigners to enter the sanctuary.

Women travellers

Outside popular tourist destinations, Indians are unaccustomed to foreigners, and they may stare or pass rude comments if they see western

Etiquette in practice

women in bathing clothes. Away from the beaches and swimming pools, women are expected to dress modestly and not wear bikinis, swimsuits, shorts and skimpy skirts. Most Indian women do not drink or smoke.

Holidays

India celebrates many holidays during which monuments and most museums, banks and shops may not be open.

Photography

Southern India is extremely photogenic, with lush hills, pretty beaches, picturesque villages, historic cities, beautiful temples and other monuments, and an abundance of wildlife. Sunny weather most of the year adds to the joy of photography in Kerala and the rest of Southern India.

It is generally better to ask before you take photographs of local people, especially women. Taking them without permission is considered rude by some, although many Indians are keen to be photographed. Children trying to get into the frame or curious people wanting to see your equipment could crowd you.

Although taking the necessary equipment with you can save some time, many shops stock extra memory, and at the main tourist sites hawkers walk around selling such supplies.

Camera thefts are common in India. Always take care of your camera, and as far as it is possible do not leave it in a hotel room or taxi.

Kerala

Forming a strip of land along the southwest coast of India, Kerala is home to a wide diversity of scenery within its narrow confines, including some of Southern India's finest beaches, the backwaters immediately inland, spice-planted midlands and the tropical forests of the Western Ghats that rise inland parallel to the coast.

The spices of Kerala attracted traders, invaders and settlers to its harbours, and these influences are reflected in the state's many historic buildings. The temples of Thiruvananthapuram, the state capital, are in the Dravida style of the Cholas who conquered Kerala in the 10th and 11th centuries, while its museums and public buildings were designed by British architects. Many of Kochi's buildings show the influences of the Portuguese, Dutch and British colonial powers, and the town is also home to the oldest intact synagogue and one of the oldest churches in Southern India. The influence of trade with the Arabs can be seen in the Islamic quarters of Kozhikode, Kannur and Kasaragode. Kerala's own distinct identity is best explored in its heartland – Kottayam district, with its Syrian Christian churches, wooden plantation houses and beautifully painted Keralan temples, and Thrissur district, which has holy temples as well as a number of important institutions for the dance

dramas of Kerala and the classical music of Southern India.

For decades, chartered flights have landed at Thiruvananthapuram because of its proximity to Kovalam, which is now seeing an upmarket renewal with luxury resorts developing along its beaches, as well as further south at Chowara and Poovar. North of Thiruvananthapuram, the historic towns of Kollam, Alappuzha and Kottayam offer access to the backwaters, a special attraction of Kerala. Connected by canals, the backwaters are navigable waterways that pass through a lush green landscape of plantations, villages, fishermen and waterfront markets. For many travellers, a night on board a houseboat, or a sunset boat trip, is a highlight of their stay in Southern India.

The stretch of coast north of Kochi is less visited than the southern districts, but it is now seeing increased tourist development, with resorts growing up along the beaches and backwaters near the great fort of Bekal, the historic city of Kozhikode and the historic town of Kannur.

Running parallel to the coast, the Western Ghats are richly forested and are also planted with tea, coffee and spices. One of the most popular destinations in these hills is Periyar Lake, where tigers, elephants, sloth bears, wild dogs and other wildlife arrive to drink at the lakefront from the surrounding forests. Munnar, the main hill resort of Kerala, is about 1,500m (5,000ft) above sea level amid a dramatic landscape of tea plantations, high peaks, stunningly beautiful lakes and wildlife-rich forests. In the past, the barrier formed by the Western Ghats protected much of Kerala from invaders, with the exception of aggressors from Tamil Nadu and Karnataka, who entered through the Palghat (or Palakkad) Gap. Near the gap are the rainforests of the Silent Valley and the Annamalai hills.

Across the Palakkad Gap, the hills of the Wayanad district are the setting for attractive waterfalls and wildlife reserves that are contiguous with those of Karnataka and Tamil Nadu.

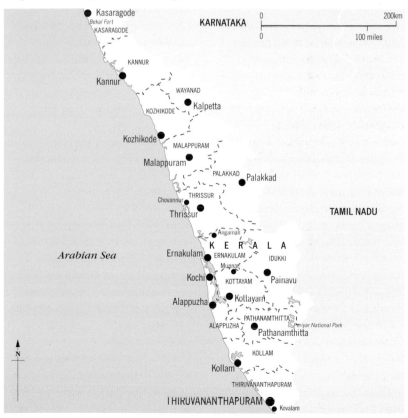

THIRUVANANTHAPURAM
Thiruvananthapuram city

The capital of Kerala, Thiruvananthapuram's history dates from the medieval Venadu dynasty that reigned over the kingdom of Travancore from Padmanabhapuram between 1550 and 1750. In 1750, Raja Marthanda Varma dedicated his kingdom to Padmanabha, a form of Lord Vishnu, and declared himself a slave of the deity. The capital of Travancore was moved to Thiruvananthapuram, literally 'the city of the sacred serpent'.

This was a far-sighted move that ensured the support of the military and the respect of his subjects for his dynasty. Irrigation schemes were introduced and Thiruvananthapuram became an important centre for the salt trade. Raja Marthanda Varma established ties with the Dutch, and also with the British who emerged as the major power in Kerala. The British intervened in the internal affairs of Travancore, when Diwan Thampi plotted against them, and under successive Maharanis, Laxmi and Parvati, the state prospered. The chief minister of Maharani Laxmi was Colonel Munro, a British officer who established public services including healthcare and education. Substantial irrigation works were undertaken and many other significant developments took place.

The golden age of Travancore was from 1829 when Swami Tirunal, son of Maharani Laxmi, proved to be an exceptional ruler, initiating wide-ranging reforms in social matters, administration, economic systems, arts and education.

Following public petitions, Thiruvananthapuram formed a legislative council in 1888, and in the 20th century opened its temples to Hindus of all castes. It was the hub of activity during the Civil Disobedience Movement against the British.
Thiruvananthapuram is 220km (137 miles) from Kochi and 382km (237 miles) from Kozhikode, with good rail connections with Madgaon (Goa) and other parts of India. Thiruvananthapuram also has an international airport. The tourist office is at Park View near the museums.

Padmanabhaswamy Temple

Raja Marthanda Varma rebuilt this temple in 1733, and it is said to house an idol found in the hills around Thiruvananthapuram. Unusually for Kerala, the architecture is predominantly Dravidian, with an intricately carved seven-storeyed *gopuram* (towering gatehouse) behind a temple tank. The interior of the temple is usually open only to Hindus, but foreign visitors can request permission to visit in order to see the murals, sculptures and the columns supporting the main pavilions. The central shrine has images of Vishnu, Brahma and Shiva.

1km (²/₃ mile) southwest of Trivandrum Station. Tel: 0471 245 0233. Open: daily 4.15–5.15am, 6.45–7.30am, 8.30–10.30am, 11.30–11.45am & 5.15–7.30pm. If granted permission to enter the temple, visitors are required to wear white sarongs (dhotis) for men and sarees for women.

Puthe Maliga Palace

Sometimes pronounced Puthen Malika Palace and also called Kuthira Maliga Palace, this building was built in the 19th century by Maharajah Swami Tirunal. The name is derived from the frieze of wooden horses and literally means the 'palace of horses'. Made from teak and rosewood, with granite columns and marble interiors, the palace houses music halls, reading rooms, an excellent library, European mirrors and chandeliers, weapons, crystal and ivory thrones, Kathakali idols, elephant howdahs (seats laid across elephant backs) and other princely memorabilia. The palace is also renowned for hosting a classical music festival in January or February each year.

Immediately to the east of Padmanabhaswamy Temple, or 900m (984yds) southwest of Trivandrum Station. Tel: 0471 247 3952. Open: Mon–Sat 8.30am–1pm, 3–5.30pm. Small admission charge.

KALARIPAYATTU

This martial art is said to have evolved during the battles between the Cheras and the Cholas in the 9th and the 12th centuries. The Kalaripayattu martial techniques became popular in the 12th century when feudal lords of the principalities that comprised medieval Kerala were constantly at war with each other. Arenas called kalaris were set up to train warriors for combat (payattu is the Malayalam word for combat). Each village had a kalari, near the local temple and sacred pond, which ensured a combination of health, fitness, defence, religion and hygiene. The kalari itself comprised a gymnasium, a temple and educational facilities. A trainer, called the Gurukkal, was responsible for the martial training, education and health of each member of the kalari. Training was so effective in producing skilled warriors that the British banned the kalari system in 1792, and the practice of Kalaripayattu had almost died out by the 19th century.

Training traditionally begins at the age of eight and can continue for a decade. Students are trained in the art of using wooden weapons such as the cheruvate (a short stick), kettukara (long stick) and ottakal (a wooden club). Ankatari is the technique of duelling with metal weapons, including swords, shields, spears and daggers. The most dreaded kalari weapon is the umurio sword, and training in the use of this sword is generally given only to a potential Gurukkal, as it is a lethal weapon.

Oil massages, traditionally used to increase the suppleness of the body, have now developed into a branch of Ayurveda. The martial art sequences of Kalaripayattu are said to have been adopted into the martial arts of other countries.

At Thiruvananthapuram's CVN Kalari (Tel: 0495 239 1808), the Gurukkal trains students in armed and unarmed combat. Another important academy for martial arts is Balacharan Nair Kalari, outside the city centre. The Kalari welcomes visitors and can arrange demonstrations.

Walk: Colonial Trivandrum

Thiruvananthapuram, previously known as Trivandrum, was strongly influenced by the Raj, with Maharani Laxmi appointing a British officer as the minister. As part of its colonial legacy, Thiruvananthapuram has a park with museums, art galleries and a zoo, and the cantonment area called Palayam with old administrative buildings, churches and markets.

Allow about 4 hours, including sightseeing, plus some time to browse and shop at Connemara Market.

Start at the main gate. Vehicles are not allowed inside and can be left at the paid parking area in a lane nearby. To the right inside the Botanical and Zoological Park entrance are the Chitra Enclave and art galleries displaying the collections of artists such as K C S Panikar, as well as temporary exhibitions. The centrepiece of the park is the Arts and Crafts Museum. To reach the Arts and Crafts Museum, do not enter the park, instead turning right into the museum compound.

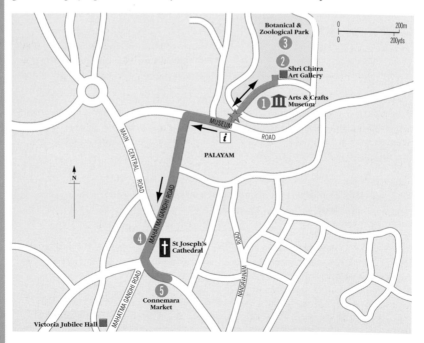

1 Arts and Crafts Museum

Formerly called the Napier Museum, this government arts museum was established in 1856. The colourful façade has European, Indo-Saracenic, Keralan and Chinese Pagoda features. The museum has an excellent collection of 12th-century bronzes, 15th-century woodcarvings, temple chariots, gold jewellery, Javanese objects, Kathakali figures and a model of the Guruvayur temple. To the east is the Natural History Museum, which houses a model of a Nair *Tharawad* (wood and stucco house), and explains the different parts of a *Nalakettu*, a traditional courtyard house of Kerala.
Open: Tue, Thur–Sun 10am–4.45pm, Wed 1–4.45pm. Small admission charge.
To the north of the Arts and Crafts Museum is the Shri Chitra Art Gallery. Cross back over the road and enter the Park. The gallery is to the right.

2 The Shri Chitra Art Gallery

This gallery exhibits a collection of Raja Ravi Varma's portraiture, as well as a variety of works of Rajasthani, Tanjore, Balinese, Mughal, Chinese, Japanese, Tibetan Buddhist and South Indian art.
Open: Tue, Thur–Sun 10am–4.45pm, Wed 1–4.45pm. Small admission charge.
Explore the Botanical and Zoological Park.

RAVI VARMA'S PAINTINGS

Raja Ravi Varma (1848–1906) was one of India's first artists to take up oil painting, to master perspective and to use human models for Hindu deities. He was awarded the Vira Sanghala Decoration by the state of Travancore.

3 Botanical and Zoological Park

Established in 1859, this park is worth visiting for its zoo, which is one of the largest in India. The botanical garden has many interesting trees and plants.
Tel: 0471 231 6275; museumzoo@ sancharnet.in. Open: 9am–4.45pm. Admission charge.
From the Zoological Park gate, follow the path alongside the Arts and Crafts Museum to the main gate, then turn right and walk past the tourist office, turning left down Mahatma Gandhi Road. You will pass St Joseph's Cathedral on your left, and see the Victoria Jubilee Hall in the distance.

4 St Joseph's Cathedral

This 19th-century cathedral is one of the oldest churches in Thiruvananthapuram, with a tall tower and a red-brick façade showing Gothic influences. The church has some interesting British tombstones to the rear.
Services in English at 5.45am daily.
Turn left at the gate and continue along Mahatma Gandhi Road. Connemara Market is on your left, just off the main road.

5 Connemara Market

This recently renovated market has a granite entrance and overhanging roofs supported by brackets.
Retrace your steps to the car park off Museum Road, or take public transport from the market entrance.

Thiruvananthapuram environs

Situated along the coast where the Western Ghats come fairly close to the sea, Thiruvananthapuram is the starting point for trips to lesser-known beaches and minor hill stations. The excursions are good options for those who want to get away from the crowds of the state capital city and the travellers' scene at nearby Kovalam (*see p32*). As the southernmost district of Kerala, Thiruvananthapuram also makes a good base for trips across the Tamil Nadu border.

Kariavattom

North of Thiruvananthapuram, Kariavattom is home to Kerala University and the Technopark, a computing and business centre. The university library has a superb collection of palm-leaf manuscripts in numerous languages, besides copper inscriptions and paper manuscripts, initiated by the Travancore Princely State.
15km (9 miles) from Thiruvananthapuram.
University library. Tel: 0471 247 7844. Usually open from 10am–4pm Mon–Fri except during the university's holidays.

Nedumangad

The renovated **Koyikkal Palace** (*Tel: 0472 281 2136; Archadd@ sancharnet.in. Admission charge*) at Nedumangad has a folklore museum containing musical instruments and folk arts, and a fine coin collection.

About 18km (11 miles) north of Thiruvananthapuram. Open: 9am–5pm. Closed: Mon.

Neyyar Lake

Neyyar Lake is the focal point of the 128sq km (49sq mile) **Neyyar Wildlife Sanctuary**. Here you are likely to see elephants, tigers, bear, gaur, deer and wild boar, but be warned – they are hard to spot. The higher ranges are covered by grassland inhabited by the tahr (a goat-like mammal) and other herbivores, but trekking permits are essential. There is a lion safari park, where some lions can be seen in an enclosure, and a crocodile park.

The **Sivananda Yoga Vendanta Dhanwantari Ashram** (*Tel: 0471 227 3093; yogaindia@sivananda.org*) overlooks Neyyar Lake and conducts yoga classes for beginners, advanced students and teachers.

The Agastya Hills, some of the highest in southern Kerala at 1,869m (6,230ft), can be seen from the lake on a clear day.
About 32km (20 miles) east of Thiruvananthapuram. Buses leave from the KSRTC Thampanoor stand in Thiruvananthapuram.
Neyyar Sanctuary. Tel: 0471 232 2217. wildlife@sify.com.

Padmanabhapuram Palace

This seat of power of Travancore State is now officially in Tamil Nadu. The name literally refers to the lotus emerging from the navel of Lord Vishnu to whom this palace was dedicated by Raja Marthanda Varma. The palace was the residence and administrative headquarters of the Venadu dynasty before they moved to Thiruvananthapuram in 1750, and its oldest parts probably date from the 1550s. Built from teak and supported by granite, it is an excellent example of Keralan architecture, showing the woodcarving that has been characteristic of Kerala's art, as well as some fine murals and well-sculpted stone figures.

The palace comprises the royal dwelling quarters, the administrative areas, public spaces and a shrine. The interior is exquisite, especially the entrance hallway with its carved rosewood ceilings, and the Durbar hall that has floors finished with crushed shells, egg whites, coconuts and juices, and windows adorned with coloured mica.

About 63km (39 miles) southeast of Thiruvananthapuram, on the road to Kanyakumari. Open: Tue–Sun 9am–5pm. Nominal admission charge, camera and video charges.

Wildlife at Neyyar Lake

Ponmudi

At an altitude of over 1,000m (3,281ft), Ponmudi is a lightly wooded hill resort. Banana, rubber, spice and tea plantations can be seen on the road up from Thiruvananthapuram, and the area is well known for its pleasant walks. *65km (40 miles) from Thiruvananthapuram.*

Varkala

Varkala is a town with a famous Krishna Temple, Janardhana Temple, which was largely rebuilt in the 13th century, while the subsidiary shrines are said to be older than the temple itself. There are Saivite shrines outside the main complex, and on the cliff near the temple is the old palace of the Travancore Princely State, which has been converted into a government guesthouse (*Tel: 0470 260 2227*). Another attraction is Papanasam Beach at Varkala, which has been developed into a popular resort. *55km (34 miles) north of Thiruvananthapuram.*

Veli Beach

Veli has been developed as a tourist park along the shores of a lagoon stretching out to sea, and ending in a sandbar and a good beach with boating facilities. The landscaped gardens of the park contain fine sculpture by Canai Kunuram, known for their balance, harmony and erotic elements. *9km (5¹/₂ miles) from Thiruvananthapuram.*

KOVALAM

Kovalam was the beach resort of the Maharajas of Travancore. Western tourists discovered its charms in the 1960s and 1970s when, like Goa, it became a 'hippy hang-out' and started attracting backpackers and package holidaymakers. Today, Kovalam is one of Kerala's most popular tourist destinations and it rates among India's most visited beach resorts.

Aruvipuram

Literally 'the village of flowing waters', Aruvipuram on the **River Neyyar** attracts many pilgrims for ritual bathing, since the pilgrims believe that the river waters have healing properties. Pilgrims usually use the steps to wash their feet, but the waters are torrential so swimming is unsafe.
20km (12 miles) south of Thiruvananthapuram.

Beaches

Kovalam's main claim to fame is its four stretches of beach, separated from one another by rocky promontories or streams. Most of the tourists visit **Hawah Beach** (or Eve's Beach), and **Lighthouse Beach** near the striking red-and-white lighthouse on the headland. **Samudra Beach**, about 4km (2½ miles) north, is becoming an increasingly popular option. Some 8km (5 miles) south of Kovalam, beaches like **Chowara** and **Pullukudi** are gaining popularity as alternatives. Chowara is home to some of Kerala's best-known Ayurvedic centres.

Kanyakumari

A visit to Kanyakumari, the southern tip of India, undoubtedly forms the most popular day excursion from Kovalam. Kanyakumari means 'virgin maiden' and refers to Devi Karna who sought to become Shiva's consort by doing penance at the tip of India. When she was unsuccessful, Devi Karna proclaimed she would remain a virgin. The temple to Devi Karna is the site of one of the most important pilgrimages for Hindus. Devotees consider her to be the protector of the Indian shores. The **Vivekanand Memorial** is situated on a rock offshore from the mainland and gives spectacular views; it is dedicated to Swami Vivekanand who visited in 1892 as a devotee of the virgin goddess and stayed on to meditate. Inspired by his meditation, Swami Vivekanand spoke at the Parliament of Religions at Chicago and founded the Ramkrishna Mission at Chennai. The memorial built in 1970 integrates temple architectural styles from different parts of India.
86km (53 miles) southeast of Thiruvananthapuram.

Neyyattinkara

The **Shri Krishna Temple** at this site dates from the 18th century; Raja Marthanda Varma is said to have stayed here.
The town is 20km (12 miles) from Thiruvananthapuram on National Highway 47. There is a holy bathing

The coast at Kovalam – an earthly paradise

site on the Neyyar River about 4km (2¹/₂ miles) from the town.

Padmanabhapuram

See pp30–31.

Suchindram

Unusually, the temple at Suchindram is shared by the trinity of Vishnu, Brahma and Shiva. The temple has an ornately decorated towering *gopuram* (temple gatehouse), and to the north is an enormous tank with a shelter in the middle. Founded during the Pandiyan reign, which reached its zenith in the 12th and 13th centuries and expanded under the Nayakas of Thirumalai in the 17th century, the temple became part of the Travancore Princely State and houses treasures from different kingdoms. Among the interesting sculptures are those depicting Shiva, his consort and sons, as well as a towering Hanuman statue inside.

14km (9 miles) from Kanyakumari. Open: daily 3am–1pm, 4–8pm. Usually open to non-Hindus. Sunset ceremonies on Friday.

Vizhinjam

This was the capital of the Ay rulers who were a dominant force in Travancore's history. Once controlled by the Pandiyans in the 7th century, the Ay rulers rose to prominence 200 years later. Now largely a fishing village, Vizhinjam has an 8th-century shrine with figures cut into the rock.

3km (2 miles) from Kovalam.

The home of Ayurveda

Ayurveda probably started in the Himalayas in about the 6th century BC, and is a type of herbal medicine which is used in most parts of India. It is associated with Kerala on account of the many colleges and hospitals, such as the one at Kottakal, and the many Ayurvedic resorts that have recently become established in the state. The word Ayurveda is derived from the Sanskrit words for 'wisdom', or 'science', or 'life', and the philosophy is based on a holistic understanding of the human body, mind and spirit; illness affects both the body and the mind, and these should therefore not be treated separately. Physical and emotional health can be maintained by balancing energies, and diagnosis is based on the philosophy that illness is the result of a loss of balance of *doshas*, a combination of elements that comprise the human body, making use of the 107 *marmas* or sensitive points. Ayurvedic physicians prescribe traditional healing techniques such as purification, diet, herbal medicine, massage, meditation and yoga.

Ayurveda was discouraged by the British Raj, but following

Dhara – an Ayurvedic treatment involving a flow of herbal oil onto the patient's forehead

independence in 1947 the government of India promoted Ayurveda as an important form of medicine.

For most visitors to Kerala, the most enjoyable and relaxing Ayurvedic treatment is a massage, which is also the first cleansing therapy offered to most patients as a form of pre-detoxification. The massage oils have properties that help to heal and protect the skin; the therapist uses gentle, circular movements – with the degree of pressure depending on the patient's condition – covering the head and the body, and the massage is followed by a steam bath. Some resorts also offer synchronised massages by two or more therapists, as well as Chavatti-Uzhichil, which is done by foot instead of by hand, for rejuvenation, muscle toning, weight loss and improved circulation.

The Ayurvedic programmes offered by most hotels and resorts are *Rasayana Chikitsa* (rejuvenation therapy), *Kayakalpa Chikitsa* (body immunisation and longevity therapy), *Sveda Karma* (involving body cleansing by inducing perspiration as part of pre-detoxification) and *Panchakarma* (for overall wellbeing). Many resorts provide programmes for patients suffering from rheumatic and arthritic problems, backaches and chronic ailments. Meditation, yoga and stress-relief programmes are also popular.

The treatments on offer at Ayurvedic resorts include the following:

Dhara: In Sirodhara, a thin flow of herbal oil, from a pot with a hole suspended over the patient's head, is directed to a spot on the forehead near the eyebrows and then stroked down the hair by the therapist and allowed to permeate the skin. The oil may be massaged into the scalp if prescribed by the physician. Other forms of *dhara* involve the pouring of buttermilk, fermented yoghurt-based fluids or medicated milk over the forehead or body.

Karnapoornam: Ear treatment.

Marma Kizhi: Massage with herbal powder-filled cloth bags.

Nasyam or Nasya Karma: Nasal therapy, which involves inhaling medicated vapours.

Pizhichil: A herbal compress.

Sirolepam: Application of herbal pastes chosen for the patient.

Snehapanam: Administers ghee internally for patients of osteoarthritis, leukaemia and other ailments.

Sveda: Induces perspiration by application of herbal bundles, along with medicated steam baths or herbal tub baths.

Tharpanam and Ajanam: Eye treatments.

Udvarthanam: Herbal powder massage.

Urovasti: Administration of oil to the chest.

KOLLAM
Kollam town

Surrounded by coconut palm and cashew plantations, the market town of Kollam, or Quilon, is situated on the edge of Ashtamudi Lake. As one of the gateways to the waterways of Kerala, Kollam was an important trading city coveted by colonial powers, and some of its old, red-tiled wooden houses still line the narrow, winding streets.

Known to Marco Polo as Koilum, it traded with Europe, the Middle East and China, and evidence of Chinese connections still survives in its ceramics and in the style of fishing nets lining the backwaters.

In the 9th century, Kollam was the capital of the Venadu Dynasty; today it is known as a convenient staging post for boat trips on the backwaters.

Kollam is 61km (38 miles) northwest of Thiruvananthapuram, 119km (74 miles) from Kochi and 280km (174 miles) from Kozhikode, with good road and rail connections.

Ashtamudi Lake

Literally 'seven creeks', Ashtamudi Lake extends north from Kollam. It is an attractive lake with palm-fringed banks and promontories extending into the water, where dugouts carry coir, copra (coconut kernel), cashew and fish. Boat tours on the canals of Ashtamudi provide a good way of experiencing village life, coir weaving, copra drying, fish and shrimp farming, matchstick making and agriculture.

5km (3 miles) northwest of central Kollam. Boats leave from the KSRTC bus stand at the southern end of the lake.

Church of Our Lady of Velankani

One of the landmark buildings of Kollam, this is an unusual-looking Christian shrine, in the shape of a pyramid and topped by a golden virgin.

Situated near Alappuzha Road.

Mukkada Bazaar

The series of parallel streets that make up the bazaar are teeming with spice warehouses, metal merchants and rope makers plying their trade. The best time to go is late afternoon.

South of Main Street.

KETTUVALAMS

Kettuvalams are strong and sturdy boats capable of carrying heavy loads. Often called rice boats, the Kettuvalams are used for cargo and as a means of transport, and they are made from wooden planks tied together with coir and coconut fibre, with a thatched roof to protect people and cargo from the rain. In deep water the boatman uses an oar to propel the boat along, but in shallower water he uses a long bamboo pole, rather like the sort used in a punt.

The Kettuvalam declined in importance when road transport began to make most of the waterways redundant, but today many of them have been redesigned and remodelled as passenger boats and houseboats (*see p130*).

Kollam environs

Kayyamkulam

Some 33km (21 miles) north of
Kollam, Alamakadavu on the outskirts
of Kayyamkulam is a centre for the
construction of Kerala's rice boats,
called *Kettuvalams* (*see opposite*).

Krishnapuram Palace

Raja Marthanda Varma built this
palace near Kayyamkulam in the
18th century, probably expanding
older royal residences that existed here.
Renovated in 1999, the two-storey
palace is a good example of Keralan
architecture, with gabled roofs and
woodcarvings, and it still has its
original bathing tank inside. The palace
contains the mural of *Gajendra
Moksha*, one of the largest wall
paintings in Kerala, depicting the
Bhagwad story of the deliverance of the
elephant chief by Lord Vishnu.

Now a museum, the palace exhibits
sculptures and paintings from various
archaeological sites and copies
of murals from Matancherry Palace, as
well as some from other temples and
churches. One of the prized exhibits is
a palanquin (a covered seat enclosed
by curtains and carried on men's
shoulders) used by the married
women of the royal family, and an
ancient Buddha statue stands in the
landscaped garden.
*47km (29 miles) north of Alappuzha.
Tel: 0479 244 1133. Open: 10am–1pm,
2–5pm. Closed: Mon. Small admission
charge.*

Entrance to Krishnapuram Palace

Valliakvu

Also called Amritapuri, Valliakvu is
home to the ashram of Mata
Amritanandamayi (*Tel: 0476 289 7578.
www.amritapuri.org. Programme: daily
from 5am. Public darshan Wed, Thur,
Sat & Sun*), whose Mission Trust
supports a variety of projects such as
orphanages and hospitals.
12km (7 miles) south of Kayyamkulam.

ALAPPUZHA
Alappuzha town

Alappuzha, or Allepey, is a market town clustered along a network of canals. The waterways are still in use and service the coir industry that has thrived here since the 19th century. Another important industry here is cashew processing, and some of the old factories and warehouses still stand. *Alappuzha is 130km (81 miles) northwest of Thiruvananthapuram, 56km (35 miles) south of Kochi and 205km (127 miles) south of Kozhikode, with good road and rail connections.*

Temples

The **Mullakal Devi Temple** (*Muhakal Road, just south of junction with Cullan Road*) is among several that participate in a festival every December, which is celebrated with music, dance, rituals and processions. Alappuzha also has a modern **Jain Shwemtambar Temple** (*just north of South Canal, towards the beach*), built next to the older Jain shrine. *Open: daily 6–8am & 4.30–8pm.*

Alappuzha environs
Ambalapuzha

Sree Krishna Ananda Temple at Ambalapuzha is one of the most important temples of the erstwhile Travancore State. Designed in typical Keralan style, with gabled roofs and carved wooden façades, it is set beside a sacred tank. Milk rice, which is offered at the temple, is considered as the gift of a Brahmin to the poor. *About 14km (9 miles) south of the town centre.*

Aranmula

Aranmula is well known as the centre of bell-metal handicrafts, and especially for its famous mirrors. It has a Parthasarthy Temple to Lord Krishna as the charioteer for Arjuna, a central figure in the Hindu epic *Mahabharata.* Aranmala is also the site for a boat race which is more a procession than a competition, with devotees believing that Krishna is in every boat. *10km (6 miles) east of Chengannur.*

Traversing the backwaters of Alappuzha

Arthungal

The **St Sebastian Church** (*Tel: 0478 257 2374. www.arthunkalchurch.org. Open: 8am–8pm. Free admission*) at Arthungal was built in 1591 and is well known for the procession that carries the saint's statue to the beach in January. *About 25km (16 miles) north of the town centre via Mararikulam.*

Haripad

Haripad has one of Kerala's most important Subramanya Temples, which houses an idol of the four-armed deity which devotees believe was found in the river.

16km (10 miles) south of Alappuzha on National Highway 47 leading to Kollam. Haripad is one of the major centres for boat races and festivals in August and December.

Mannarsala

The **Nagaraja Temple** at Mannarsala (*Tel: 0479 241 3788. www.mannarasala.org*) is one of the most important of the many temples located in the 'snake groves' of Kerala. The surrounding woodlands have several statues of snake gods and hooded cobras among the trees and along the paths leading to the temple dedicated to the Snake King, Nagaraja. Childless women visit the shrine to pray for a child, and, if they have one, they return to donate the equivalent weight of the baby in grains to the temple.

The temple is best known for its association with the *Mahabharata* which mentions the fleeing of snakes to a place devotees believe is Mannarsala. Unusually, the temple has a priestess as the local Namboodri Brahmin women are said to have planted sacred groves for the snakes. In typical Keralan architectural style, the temple's main shrine is dedicated to Nagaraja, the serpent king, and his consort.

Thousands of Hindus attend the temple's annual festival in September or October, when its idols are carried through the woods, and offerings of milk, rice and turmeric are made. *About 32km (20 miles) south of Alappuzha.*

Mararikulam

The fishing hamlet of Mararikulam provides access to the excellent Marari Beach, which is a popular resort. *15km (9 miles) north of Alappuzha.*

BOAT RACES

On the second Saturday of August, the Nehru Boat Race at Alappuzha is one of Kerala's most famous regattas, and thousands come to watch the race on Vembanad Lake. Behind the stern of each snake boat, shaped like the hood of a cobra, a hundred or so rowers power their way across the waters, shouting and singing enthusiastically. The rowers are supported by helmsmen and women, who do the steering, and cheered by singers and spectators from their village. The crowd avidly watches a tradition that harks back to the time when the snake boats transported troops to battle.

Boat races are also a feature of the Onam celebrations elsewhere in Kerala. At Payipad near Haripad, the boat races are said to be in honour of the finding of the idol of Subhramanya at Haripad, while at Arunmala the boats carry effigies of Lord Krishna.

The backwaters of paradise

A unique aspect of Kerala's geography is its backwaters, a network of rivers, streams, lagoons, lakes, canals and tanks that runs along most of its coastline. The best-known stretch is from Kollam to Kochi, the northern section of which is called Kuttinad. The backwaters have few outlets to the sea and the lagoons depend on rivers for their water. In the monsoon season, sea water enters parts of the inland lagoons and canals: this combination of saline and fresh water is essential to the aquatic life of the backwaters, including the coveted *karimean* fish.

Touring the backwaters is one of the highlights of a visit to Kerala.

Waterfront activities like coir-making, rice-growing, toddy-tapping and fishing can be seen along the banks, and traditional dugouts ply the waterways. The banks are green with coconut palms and groves of mango, papaya, jackfruit and other trees, and tapioca is among the crops grown here. Travelling the backwaters also gives a glimpse of village life; entire settlements are located on strips of land separating the waterways, and the houses have poultry, cattle, pigs and ducks, and even vegetable gardens. Prawns and fish are farmed, sand is dredged for construction, and shells are collected for the production of lime. The boats pass canals where

A boatman cruising along the backwaters

Chinese fishing nets are a distinctive feature of the backwaters

coconuts, coir, cashews and food are loaded onto dugouts.

The most popular backwater trip is the journey from Kollam to Alappuzha, or vice versa, which takes about eight hours, usually departing at 10.30am, with halts along the way, to the coir village of Thrikkunnapuha, to islands such as Lekshmithuruthy, and to popular spots such as the ashram at Amritapuri. Shorter trips are also available from Kollam, Alappuzha and Kochi, and from the northern backwaters near Calicut and Bekal. Some cruises, such as those from Alappuzha and Kottayam, include toddy tasting in their itinerary.

Apart from tours, passenger boats and public ferries, it is also possible to hire motorboats and speedboats for travelling the backwaters. Hotels and resorts at Kottayam, Kumarakom, Alappuzha and Kollam also organise backwater cruises and short boat trips. The best, but more expensive, option is to charter a houseboat.

TROUBLED WATERS

Although travellers see a somewhat idyllic side of life on Kerala's backwaters, these areas are not free of environmental problems. Reclaimed land for agriculture has reduced the surface-water area, and almost all the mangrove vegetation has been destroyed. The construction of barriers across Vembanad Lake is one of the many changes that has affected the ecology, along with increased population density and pollution. Despite initiatives from the Ministry of the Environment, and in particular the National Mangrove Committee, and calls to action from the National Institute of Oceanography, the mangroves continue to deteriorate, with Kerala's the worst hit in the country

KOTTAYAM
Kottayam city

Kottayam is sandwiched between the hills to the east and the backwaters to the west, with fertile lands on the outskirts producing rubber and other cash crops. The Christian population of Kerala followed the Syrian Orthodox Church, but after attempts by the Portuguese to Latinise the Church, the Syrian Christians took an oath stating that the Portuguese priests were not their leaders.

The Syrian Church became an autonomous body without links to Rome. Many Syrian Christians subsequently rejoined the Roman Church after a visit by the Pope, but one group formed the Jacobite Syrian Christian Church. After independence, most of the churches reunited, and Kottayam's history of Syrian Christian settlement is reflected in its churches.

Kottayam is also known for its high literacy rate, and it publishes some of the most read Malayalam newspapers. Many well-known Malayalam writers hail from Kottayam, and a cooperative was established here in 1945.

Cheria Palli (St Mary's Church)

The elegant St Mary's Church, called Cheria Palli, is some 450 years old and is situated on top of a hill. Its interior displays some beautiful murals on the walls and ceiling, and above the altar.
2km (1¼ miles) north of the town centre. Sunday Mass at 9am.
Free admission.

Thirunakkara Shiva Temple

This temple is in typical Keralan style, with an interesting *Kootiattum*, the traditional temple theatre for religious dance drama.
Temple Road (at the junction with Azad Lane), in the centre of town. Usually open: daily 5am–noon & 5–8pm.

Valiya Palli

This church was built in the 16th century and is famous for its Persian Cross with a Pahlavi inscription next to the altar. Another cross has Syriac liturgy. There is also an unusual portrayal of St George slaying a dragon. The guest book has comments dating from 1899, and among its entries is one by an Ethiopian emperor.
2km (1¼ miles) north of the town centre. Free admission. Sunday and Wednesday Mass at 7.30am.

Kottayam environs
Chengannur

Chengannur has three interesting temples, all worth a visit – a Mahadev Temple with a theatre on an old plinth; a Bhagwati Temple, which is said to bring good fortune to devotees; and a small 18th-century Narsimha Temple.
About 30km (19 miles) south of Kottayam, 1km (⅔ mile) off the highway to Thiruvananthapuram.

Ettumanoor
See p44.

Kaviyur

Kaviyur has one of Kerala's best-preserved caves, dating from the 8th century and notable for its carved reliefs. It also houses a pillared hall, a shrine and a *linga* (a phallic image of the god Shiva).

5km (3 miles) from Thiruvalla on the rail route to Thiruvananthapuram, east of the main road.

Kumarakom

With its **bird sanctuary** (*Tel: 0481 252 5864. Open: daily 6am–5.30pm. Admission charge*), backwater villages and islands, Kumarakom has seen the development of tourist resorts around it. Here you can arrange boat trips to see the birdlife, which is at its best from November to February when migrants from the north make it their winter home. This is also a good spot to experience traditional farming life and village activities.

About 16km (10 miles) north of Kottayam. Half-hourly buses leave from the KSRTC bus stand in Kottayam for Kumarakom.

St John's Cathedral

Designed by Lauric Baker, this Syrian Christian church is built in Keralan architectural style with a tiled roof, timber ceiling and a circular interior that has no visible support. It was built to mark the anniversary of the martyrdom of St Thomas.

On the road to Thiruvalla from Kottayam. Tel: 0469 260 4933.

Thiruvalla

Thiruvalla is home to the Shri Vallabh Temple, which is noted for its night-time Kathakali performances.

South of Kottayam on the road and rail route to Thiruvananthapuram. Temple open: daily 4.30–11.30am & 5–8pm. Kathakali performances 10pm–1am.

The highly adorned altar of a Syrian Orthodox church in Kottayam

Tour: North of Kottayam

The road north from Kottayam to Kochi crisscrosses rivers and backwaters, and two of Kerala's most important temples can be seen on this route.

From Kottayam to Vaikom, via the diversion to Palai, is 67km (42 miles). Allow half a day.

Drive 12km (8 miles) north from Kottayam towards Kochi. The Shiva temple of Ettumanoor is on the right-hand side, with parking available on the road heading east to Palai.

1 Ettumanoor

The **Mahadev Temple** (*open: daily 4am–12.30pm & 5–8pm*) at Ettumanoor is one of the wealthiest in Kerala. Built in the typical Keralan style in the 16th century, the temple is noted for its woodcarvings. Beautiful murals depict Vishnu in the form of Padmanabha reclining on a serpent, and Shiva as Natraj crushing evil on the *gopuram* (gatehouse), as well as the lives of Rama and Krishna, and Shaivite figures in the halls. The murals are similar in style to those in the **Mattancherry Palace** of Kochi (*see pp52–3*). The main shrine is circular, with a conical, copper-clad interior ceiling, enclosing a square sanctuary. There is a large festival here in February or March, when gold elephant statues are put on display. *A hilly road travels east from Ettumanoor to Palai, passing rubber plantations on the way.*

2 Palai

Palai, or Pala, on the banks of the Meenachil River, is the gateway to the southern highranges of the Western Ghats. It is also an important hub for Roman Catholic Syrian Christians in India and has several important and impressive churches, one of which, **St Mary's Church of Bharanangaram**,

THE PILGRIMAGE TO SABARIMALA

Kottayam lies on the route of the famous pilgrimage to the Ayyapa Temple of Sabarimala from Thiruvananthapuram. After Kottayam comes Erumeli where thousands of pilgrims, dressed in black, worship at a mosque dedicated to Varr. From Erumeli, the 60km (38-mile) track has to be covered on foot, passing Challakayam and Pampa, with stops for ceremonies at a number of pilgrim sites en route. Pilgrims have to face a steep, two-hour jungle walk to the shrine, which is 914m (2,999ft) above sea level. Eighteen golden steps symbolise various sins, and when ascending the steps, pilgrims take an oath to give up these sins.

Those who do not want to make the entire pilgrimage can take a bus to Chalakayam and then walk 8km (5 miles) to Sabarimala.

is believed to date from the 11th century. Palai also boasts the Shrine of Kurishupalli as well as a number of old Syrian Christian houses on the rubber plantations.

Retrace your tracks from Palai to Ettumanoor, and then turn north on the road to Kochi, until you come to Vaikom.

3 Vaikom

Vaikom (*open: daily 4am–noon & 5–8pm*) is one of the holiest Shiva temples in Kerala and is enshrined in myth. The temple's present structure probably dates from the 16th century and its murals are probably 18th century. These depict Shiva, Parvati and Ganesha, Vishnu with his consort, and a number of other figures.

In 1925, the temple was one of the first to allow untouchables to visit the main sanctuary. By 1928, the Maharaja of Travancore opened temples to Hindus of all castes throughout his princely state.

The temple has a 12-day festival in November and December, with a particularly auspicious last night. Deities from nearby temples are brought here throughout the festival.

From Vaikom you can drive back to Kottayam or continue on the road to Kochi.

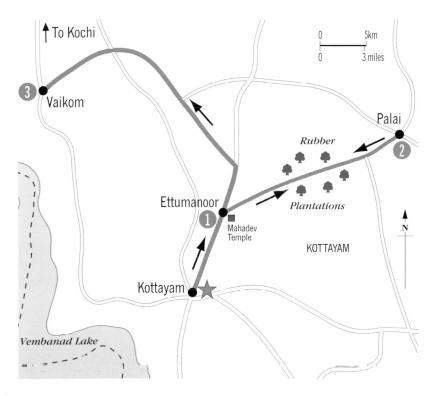

Kerala's architecture

Although centuries of maritime contact and colonisation mean that Kerala's architecture has absorbed regional and international influences, it nevertheless retains a distinctive identity. Its distinguishing features include pagoda shapes, steeply pitched sloping roofs with gables and eaves, columned galleries and open courtyards. The main building materials are grass, clay and stone, and roofs are made of timber, terracotta tiles and thatch. Flooring is usually made from clay tiles.

In some parts of Kerala, houses are made from intricately interlocked wooden grids and panels, eschewing

A museum built in Keralan style, Thiruvananthapuram

the use of a single nail or adhesives. The builders of Kerala follow directions for the correct construction of houses given by architectural treatises such as the *Vastu Shastra*, *Vastuvidya*, *Manushyalaya Chandrika*, *Vastupurusha Mandala* and the *Silparatna of Sri Kumara*: these provide instructions on the importance of location, the use of natural resources, and the various techniques for providing the best air flow, light and water storage.

Churches
Kerala's churches are generally European in style, with an elaborately decorated backdrop to the altar. Usually cruciform or rectangular, they have large halls for the congregation. Unlike temples, which are generally located near water sources for ritual bathing, most of the churches of Kerala have hilltop locations.

Mosques
The early mosques of Kerala were built in the distinctive regional style, and good examples are the 16th-century mosques of Kozhikode (Calicut). In more recent times, the mosques have adopted the Middle-Eastern model.

Nallukettu

The *Nallukettu*, or four-winged courtyard house, is probably the most beautiful garden dwelling in India and is certainly one of the country's finest examples of wooden architecture. It is centred around a sunken courtyard, which is designed to collect water, and also to ventilate the house with columned verandahs on all sides and galleries leading to the four blocks of the house. Guests are received in a reception room near the entrance and in a number of large halls which are used for entertainment. Louvred (dome-shaped) wooden ventilators and adjustable roofs ensure adequate air-flow and light, and the layout is flexible to accommodate the addition of more rooms.

The *Ettukettu* is an extended version of the *Nallukettu*, with eight blocks enclosing the courtyard. These mansions are large, with gardens, sheds, bathing ponds, wells and granaries. The *Illam* of the Namboodri Brahmins is similar to a *Nallukettu*, but is usually more compact.

Temples

Kerala's temples are rarely taller than the trees that surround them. Entered through a gatehouse called *Gopuram*, the temple has steeply pitched roofs and the interior ceiling is usually covered with copper sheaths.

The temple clusters around the main sanctum with subsidiary shrines and an entrance hall, which is called a *mandapam*. The upper parts of the sanctuary interiors are intricately decorated with carvings or paintings to denote the importance of the *Garbagriha*, home of the deity. Most temples have a theatre called the *Kootiyatram*.

A traditional Keralan lock with intricate detail

KOCHI (COCHIN)
Kochi city

With its natural harbour and setting at the entrance to the backwaters near the Arabian Sea, Kochi's rich maritime history has left an imprint on the city's architecture. After years of maritime contact with the Arabs and the Chinese, Kochi became one of India's first European colonies when the Portuguese settled here in the 16th century.

The fortunes of Kochi improved during the 16th century, when the flooding of the banks of the River Periyar created the natural harbour, while simultaneously destroying the port of Craganore that had, until then, controlled trade from central Kerala. Another stroke of luck for Kochi was the arrival of the Portuguese, who could not strike an alliance with the Zamorin, the ruler of Calicut who controlled trade between Kerala and the Middle East, and so turned their attention to Kochi. The Portuguese drew up an agreement with the Raja that helped the city grow in importance and at the same time allowed them to exploit its potential as a trading base. By 1663, the Portuguese lost their hold on the international spice market and the control of trade from Kochi passed to the Dutch.

Kochi received another boost in the 18th century when Dharma Raja, known as Raja Rama Varma of Kochi, introduced reforms and improved central administration. He also signed an alliance with the British East India Company that led to their taking over Kochi when subsequent generations proved incapable of handling the state's affairs.

When India attained independence in 1947, Kochi became one of the country's leading ports and naval bases. Today, with the eastern district of Ernakulam and numerous islands and peninsulas connected by bridges and ferries, Kochi expresses the eclecticism of Kerala, with Chinese fishing nets along the backwaters, European and Jewish buildings, and Hindu temples and mosques. Most of the old buildings are at Fort Kochi, a heritage zone, and in neighbouring Mattancherry, while Ernakulam is a dynamic district.
Kochi is 220km (137 miles) north of Thiruvananthapuram and has an airport, good rail connections to most cities in India and road access to other parts of Kerala. The Government of India tourist office is at Willingdon Island, the Kerala Tourism Development Corporation is on Shanmugham Road and the District Tourism Promotion Office is at the Old Collectorate Building, Park Avenue (Tel: 0484 236 7334).

Art galleries

The local art scene has flourished in Kochi, and art lovers have plenty of venues from which to choose.
Chitram Art Gallery, *Ma Road. Tel: 0484 309 6812. Open: daily 9.30am–8pm. Free admission.*
Kashi Art Gallery, *Burgher Street.*

Tel: 0484 221 5769. Open: Mon–Sat
10am–6pm, Sun 10am–2pm.
Free admission.
Lila Studio, Bazaar Road.
Tel: 0417 532 5963.
www.anandagaya.com;
mail@anandgaya.com. Open: Mon–Sat
10am–6pm. Closed: Sun. Free admission.

Bolghatty Island

The palatial mansion at Bolghatty was
built in 1744 when the Dutch
controlled Kochi and later became a
British residency. With its acres of
lawns and gardens, this old residency
has been converted into a resort.

Santa Cruz Basilica

This Roman Catholic church at Fort
Kochi was built in the 16th century but
had to be rebuilt in the 1800s. Notable
features include the woodcarvings and
murals inside. In 1984, Pope John Paul II
raised the church to the status of Basilica.
Near St Francis Church. Open: daily
9am–1pm & 3–5pm. English Mass Sat
6pm & Sun 4.30pm.

St Francis Church

Originally dedicated to Saint Anthony,
this is reputedly India's first European-
built church and one of the oldest
churches in Southern India. Built in
wood by Portuguese friars in 1503, the
church was rebuilt in stone later in the
same century. The oldest inscriptions
found in the church are dated to 1562.
Vasco da Gama was buried here in
1524, until, 14 years later, his remains
were shipped to Lisbon.

Rice outlets are essential to trade in Kochi

Over the years the church has experienced a number of conversions and it is now used by the Church of South India. The building is impressive and an unusual feature is its rope-operated *punkah* (fan).

Mon–Sat 10am–5.30pm, Sun after services. Free admission.

Temples

Ernakulathappan Temple in Ernakulam is known for its association with the legend of Nagarishi, who was given a snake's head as a curse for killing a snake. This legend is celebrated in January with ceremonies and cultural events.

Sixteen kilometres (10 miles) northwest from Ernakulam is the **Chottanikkara Temple**, which is a popular pilgrimage site. The main deity is worshipped as Sarasvati in the morning, Bhagwati in the afternoon and Durga in the evening, and the temple is also the site of a nine-day festival in February and March.

Erna Kulathappan Temple, Durbar Hall Road (at roundabout with Foreshaw Road), Ernakulam. Chottanikkara Temple is 16km (10 miles) northwest of Ernakulam, from where there are regular buses. Admission for Hindus only.

Vypeen

Vypeen Island is home to the Pallipuram Fort, which was built by the Portuguese in the 16th century and taken by the Dutch in 1663. The island also has a lighthouse, and its beaches are becoming increasingly popular with holidaymakers.

Vypeen Island lies 450m (492 yds) from Fort Kochi ferry jetty.

Kochi environs
Chennamangalam

Once the seat of the Palayathachan, hereditary ministers of Kochi Princely State, Chennamangalam has a 17th-century palace presented to it by the Dutch. The palace is now part of a trust that looks after 60 or so temples in and around the village.

The village also has interesting historical associations with the Jews, who built their oldest synagogue here (now largely in ruins), as well as with the Jesuit Christians and the Muslims. The 16th-century mosque still stands, but the Jesuit seminary was destroyed by Tipu Sultan.

Kodungallur, near Chennamangalam, is believed to be the port of Muziris mentioned by Pliny, and is also the place where St Thomas is said to have landed,

CHINESE FISHING NETS

Chinese fishing nets were probably introduced when Kerala traded with the Chinese court. The nets are framed with wood and strung along poles that can be 3m (10ft) long, tied to suspended boulders. The boulders help keep the net down when it is dipped into the water at high tide. Four or five men pull the net out of the water using a rope with a pulley system and rocks at the other end to balance the weight. The nets bring in large catches, and a good place to see them in action is at Kochi.

Fishermen using traditional Chinese nets can often be seen at Kochi

bringing Christianity to Kerala. Malik Bin Dinar built Kerala's first mosque, **Cheraman** (*Tel: 0480 280 3170. www.cheramanmosque.com*), at Kodungallur, and the mosque which now stands here probably dates from the 18th century.

42km (26 miles) north of Ernakulam.

Museum of Kerala History

This museum makes good use of paintings, sculptures, sound-and-light effects and audiovisual aids to depict the history of Kerala from the Neolithic period through the arrival of colonial forces to modern times.

Open: daily 10am–noon & 2–4pm. Closed: Mon and public holidays. Edapally, 10km (6 miles) north of Ernakulam towards Thrissur.

Tripunithura

Tripunithura has the **Hill Palace Museum**, with its collection of coins, manuscripts, scriptures and princely relics of Kochi and Travancore.

Hill Palace Museum, Tripunithura, Chottanikkara Road, 12km (8 miles) southeast of Ernakulam.
Tel: 0480 278 1113. Open: Tue–Sun 9am–12.30pm & 2–4pm. Small admission charge.

Walk: Mattancherry

This walk through Mattancherry, near Fort Kochi, offers an opportunity to see Kochi Synagogue, the royal palace and the Jew Town Market, a spice trade centre.

Allow 4 hours, including time for shopping.

Start at the Mattancherry Palace, which has good road and ferry access to the rest of Kochi.

1 Mattancherry Palace

Also called the Dutch Palace, this palace was actually built by the Portuguese in the 16th century and gifted to their ally, the ruler of Kochi, who gave them trading rights. The palace was completely renovated and practically rebuilt after the Dutch took over Kochi in 1663. Built on two floors around a quadrangle, the palace incorporates European influences into the traditional *Nallukettu* plan

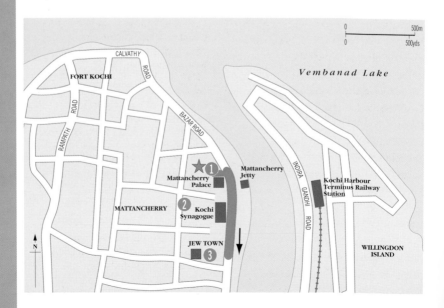

(*see p47*). It has a Bhagvati Temple in the central courtyard and Shiva and Vishnu temples to the south.

The palace has a museum of princely relics, but is known mainly for its marvellous murals depicting the entire *Ramayana* and scenes from the *Mahabharata* dating from the 16th and 17th centuries. The Central Hall was used for coronation ceremonies and has an interesting display of dresses, turbans and palanquins.

Tel: 0484 222 6085. Open: Sat–Thur 10am–5pm. Admission charge.
From the main gate of the Mattancherry Palace, head right for the synagogue.

2 Kochi Synagogue

Also called the Mattancherry Pardesi Synagogue, this was founded in 1568 and rebuilt by the Dutch in 1664, two years after the Portuguese destroyed the building. A wealthy Jewish merchant, Ezekial Rahabi, donated the clock tower in the 18th century.

Notable features include the Cantonese willow-pattern tiles, Belgian chandeliers, interlocking pews, a ladies' gallery supported by gilt columns, ornate brass pulpit and a slab from the 14th-century Kochangadi Synagogue that is now in ruins.

Open: Sun–Fri 10am–noon & 3–5pm. Admission charge.
Head south from the synagogue for the pepper exchange, established to fuel foreign investment into the spice trade.

The pepper exchange marks the start of the Jew Town Market.

3 Jew Town

The market has developed into a bazaar for antiques, curios, handicrafts and tourist souvenirs, with shops selling anything from Kathakali masks, jewel boxes and trinkets to ornate bullock carts.

From Jew Town retrace your steps along the waterfront to return to the Mattancherry Palace or to catch a ferry (from the Jetty) to Ernakulam or Kochi.

JEWRY OF KOCHI

In Jew Town you are likely to hear stories about Jews who arrived here in King Solomon's ships about the 9th century BC, those who arrived in Kerala fleeing Babylon in the 6th century BC, those who arrived from Assyria in search of refuge, as well as those who migrated to Kerala after the destruction of Jerusalem in the 1st century AD and the 10,000 Jews who fled from Palestine in the 2nd century and were allowed to settle at Muziris (probably Kodungallur).

Ideal go-betweens for the local Malayalam population and overseas traders, Jews became one of Kerala's most influential communities. Raja Bhaskara Ravi Varma, who ruled in the 10th and 11th centuries, granted the Jewish community the village of Anjuvaddam and its surrounding land. By the 16th century the Arabs and Portuguese had all but destroyed the Jewish community in Kerala, who then moved to Kochi and were granted protection, land and titles. Their population was augmented by those fleeing persecution in Europe.

The Jewish population dwindled with the mass migration to Israel in the 20th century, and today only a few Jewish families live in Kochi.

THRISSUR
Thrissur city

Thrissur is an abbreviation of Thiru, Shiva and Perur, meaning 'the city named after Lord Shiva', and for centuries it has been an important religious and cultural centre. Widely regarded as Kerala's cultural capital, Thrissur District is famous for its temples, churches, arts colleges and training schools for southern Indian performing arts.

Located at the western end of the Palakad Gap, or Palghat Pass, Thrissur formed a vital link between the coast and the interior of the peninsula. The Rajas of Central Kerala reigned from here before moving their capital to Kochi. Thrissur fell to the Zamorin of Malabar, then Sultan Hyder Ali, and eventually to the European colonial powers.

Thrissur has good road and rail connections to Thiruvananthapuram, Kozhikode and Kochi. The tourist information offices are at the Government Guest House and near the Town Hall.

Our Lady of Lourdes Cathedral

This cathedral has an impressive Indo-European façade with pink spires. The interior of the cathedral has an attractive underground shrine.

Open: daily 6.30am–6.30pm. Free admission. About 1km (²⁄₃ mile) out of the town centre towards Peechi.

Vadakkunnathan Temple

Traditionally this temple on a hillock is regarded as the centre of Thrissur, with roads radiating on all sides. The temple is an excellent example of Kerala's architecture, with fine woodcarvings decorating the roof and façade. Predominantly a Shiva Temple, it also has shrines to other deities. The main sanctuaries are dedicated to Shiva as Vadakkunnathan, and to Sankara Narayan, with a Ganesh shrine between them. The interior has beautiful murals near the main shrines. Entry is for Hindus only, but visitors are usually allowed on special days, including the famous Pooram Festival.

Tel: 0487 242 6040. Open: daily 4–10.30am & 5–8.30pm.

Thrissur environs
Angamali

This is an important Syrian Christian centre and it was once home to one of the most important bishoprics in Kerala. Nearby, at Akaparambhu, the church of Mar Sabore and Afroth was founded in the 9th century, although the present structure dates from after the 16th century and shows some Portuguese influences. It is particularly noted for its murals narrating stories from the Bible.

32km (20 miles) south of Thrissur on National Highway 47 to Ernakulam.

Guruvayoor

Guruvayoor, on the coast 16km (10 miles) northwest of Thrissur, is an important religious centre for the worship of the infant Krishna. According to one of the legends associated with the temple, the site was selected by Guru, preceptor of the gods, and Vayu, lord of the winds, when they met Lord Shiva and Parvati with Parsurama, creator of Kerala, at the tank of Guruvayoor. The tank has a statue of Krishna playing the flute. The temple has carved columns, a tall gold flagpost, called the *dhvajastambha*, a lamp tower, some murals and the image of a four-armed Krishna with a conch, a discus, a mace and a lotus.

The 16th-century poet Narayana Bhattatiri wrote the famous Hindu text *Narayaneeyam* (inspired by the Bhagwad) at Guruvayoor. A sufferer of rheumatic illness, he was cured during his visit to Guruvayoor, and since then the temple is regularly visited by people with rheumatism seeking recovery through the blessings of the infant Krishna. The temple is also a popular location for marriage ceremonies.

Our Lady of Lourdes Metropolitan Cathedral, Thrissur

Temple offerings at Guruvayoor temple

The temple elephants are housed at the Punnathur Kotha, an old fortified complex. This is a good place to see the elephants being bathed by the *mahouts* (drivers), but visitors must be careful, as the animals can be dangerous, especially the males during the breeding season. Wild elephants are brought here to be tamed for the temple festivals.
Tel: 0487 255 6335.
www.guruvayurdevaswom.org;

devaswom.gurhvayur@gmail.com.
Open: daily 3am–12.30pm &
4.30–9.15pm. Opening times may vary.
Non-Hindus are not permitted to enter.
Regular buses from Thrissur to the bus
station east of the temple.

Irinjalakuda
Irinjalakuda's **Natana Kairali Research and Performing Centre** is dedicated to the performance, preservation, documentation and promotion of

Kerala's performing arts, particularly Kuttiyam (theatre), Nangiar Koothu (solo performance) and puppetry. Performances are held here from time to time, especially during the centre's 12-day annual festival.

The **Koodalmanikyam Temple** at Irinjalakuda is an unusual temple dedicated to Rama's brother Bharata, and depicting his joy when he learned of the victory of Rama and his reunion with Sita. Irinjalakuda is also home to the **Church of St Thomas**, an impressive building erected in 1917 on the site of an older church which was built here in 1845. In January the images of saints are taken out in procession, accompanied by firework displays.

16km (10 miles) south of Thrissur.
For information about courses at Natana Kairali Research & Performing Centre for Traditional Arts contact the director at Venu G, Natana Kairali, Ammanur Chakyar Madhom, Irinjalakuda 680121. Tel: 0480 282 5559.
natanakairali@gmail.com

Kalady

Kalady, by the River Periyar, is the birthplace of Sankaracharya, one of the most important philosophers in India. In the 8th century, Sankaracharya founded the Advaita Vedanta, which has spread throughout Southern India and to other parts of the country. Kalady has two shrines in his memory, as well as a tower with details about his life and the Advainta ways of worship.
10km (6 miles) northeast of Kochi.

Kerala Kalamandalam

Founded in the 1920s and 1930s by the poet Vellathol Menon and his associate Mukunda Raja, this is an important academy for teaching the performing arts of Kerala, particularly Kathakali, Mohiniattam, Kuttiyattam and Onam Thullal. The centre is credited with the revival of Kerala's dance forms and for opening its doors to Hindus and non-Hindus alike, and it has also established international links for the promotion of Kathakali overseas. Located 16km (10 miles) north of Thrissur in Cheruthuruthy, the campus's pleasant buildings include a theatre which is designed in the style of the performing halls of Kerala's temples.
Tel: 0488 4262 418.
www.kalamandalam.org.
Open: 9am–noon & 2–5pm on working days. The office can give information on the performances and courses on offer. Send an email to info@kalamandalam.org for interaction with the masters and for information on courses at Kerala Kalamandalam.

Megalith sites

Huge stone monuments are among the earliest evidence of settlement in Kerala. Some of the best megalithic sites are located near Guruvayoor, while Chovannur has a sizeable number of the 'hat-stones' (locally called *topi-kals*) that are distinctive Iron-Age megalithic remains. Substantial remnants of Kerala's megalithic era can also be seen at Porkalam, near Thrissur.

Classical dances

Southern India is known for its living tradition of classical dances. The most popular is probably the Bharatanatyam of Tamil Nadu, which is a graceful and highly stylised form of dance usually performed by women. It combines music, gestures and mime with pure dance and expression, usually on themes of true love. A traditional recital begins with a floral offering to a deity and the first section of the performance is the *Alarippu*, which is based on the rhythm of drum beats and the vocals

Traditional Keralan dancers

of the conductor. The central section is *Varnam*, which is physically and emotionally demanding as the dancer shows her skill, dancing to the rhythm, moods and music. The final stage, called *Tillana*, shows the dancer reverting to rhythm as the performance nears its end with a concluding prayer.

The main elements of Kathakali are the sung narrative, the accompaniment of percussion instruments and the danced mime. The performer uses a variety of gestures and steps to portray the narrative, which is sung as the background theme of the performance. Boys are recruited at a very young age and spend seven or more years learning the *mudras*, hand and finger gestures and movements of the neck, head, tongue, eyes, feet, toes, arms and hands.

Mohiniattam, the dance of the enchantress, is a sensuous solo female performance that evokes the mood of love. The dance is dedicated to the female incarnation of Vishnu, Mohini the enchantress, who gives pleasure to the virtuous and brings destruction to the immoral.

Kuchipudi is a dance form of Andhra that is similar to Bharatanatyam and follows the Natya Shastras very closely. It is generally considered a folk idiom that is freer and more flexible than most other classical dance forms of Southern India. The dance drama presents an episode or a series of episodes, usually from Hindu epics, and usually performed by a group of men (though there are also solo versions). As well as mime and pure dance, Kuchipudi may also use speech in the drama.

Ottan Thulal is a male solo performance that depicts topical issues. Its simplicity, humour and satire have made it a popular art in Kerala. The dancer enacts the script with gestures, movements and expression.

Koothu, a solo performance, and Koothiattam (sometimes spelt Koodiattam), a group performance, are ancient Sanskrit dramas believed to be the inspiration behind the growth of dance dramas like Kathakali in Kerala. The Krishnanattam, patronised by the Raja Manaveda, the Zamorin of Kozhikode in the mid-17th century, has become a ritual dance at the Krishna temple of Guruvayoor, enacting the life of Krishna. Ramanattam is a similar performance, dedicated to the life of Rama.

Yakshagana from Karnataka is as much a musical play as a dance. The troupe dons elaborate make-up and costumes for the drama, which also allows the performers to speak and develop dialogue.

PERIYAR

Periyar National Park is one of Kerala's most popular tourist destinations. The reserve's artificial lake was created in 1895 by British engineers in order to irrigate Madurai and Ramanathapuram districts and to provide water to the city of Madurai. The dam submerged prime forests but resulted in the Maharaja of Travancore protecting the richly vegetated hills adjoining the lake.

Periyar is 110km (69 miles) from Kochi. There is a tourist information office at Aranya Niwas in the park (Tel: 0486 922 2023. aranyanivas@sancharnet.in), and the Wildlife Preservation Officer at Thekkady (Tel: 0486 923 2027) can be contacted for details about viewing facilities.

Periyar Tiger Reserve

This sanctuary was established by the Travancore State in 1934 and became part of 'Project Tiger' in 1973. Although Periyar is a tiger reserve, it is more famous for its elephants, which can be seen from the tourist launches which operate two-hour trips on the lake. Elephants come to the lake to drink and to feed on the marshy grasslands. Gaur (Indian bison), sambar, wild boar and Nilgiri langur are common sightings, and lucky visitors may also see sloth bear, dhole (wild dog), otters and the endangered lion-tailed macaque. This is a good spot for birdwatching, with species such as darter, cormorant, osprey, stork and kingfisher.

Guided nature treks depart from the information centre and last about three hours. On these treks you are likely to see barking deer, Malabar giant squirrels, monkeys such as langur and bonnet macaques, great and grey hornbills, grey jungle fowl, mynahs, orioles, racket-tailed drongos and monitor lizards. Some tourists come face to face with elephant herds, and watchtowers and viewing platforms can also be used, for a fee.

More serious treks, such as the Tiger Trails (an eco-development project), are also possible and include camping and staying at watchtowers in the forests. These treks cover habitats like the grasslands, where the mega-herbivores are usually seen, the moist deciduous forests and the semi-evergreen and evergreen forests. Tiger and panther sightings are rare, but visitors can see a number of other mammals, as well as an interesting variety of birds and butterflies.

Periyar Tiger Reserve. Tel: 0486 922 4571. www.periyartigerreserve.org; mail@periyartigerreserve.org. Admission charge.

Two-hour launch cruises, called boat safaris, depart from the jetty at regular intervals. The first cruise runs from 7–9am, and the last from 4–6pm. The guided nature trek starts at 7am.

Plantations

Some spice plantations near Periyar Tiger Reserve welcome visitors, and tourist offices, spice shops and some hotels run guided tours to the cardamom, rubber and coffee plantations of Murikkady, the pepper plantations at Vandiperiyar and the cardamom centre at Vandanmedu. Peermade (sometimes spelt Pirmed), on the road from Kottayam to Kumily leading to Periyar Tiger Reserve, has a number of picturesquely located tea, rubber and cardamom plantations. *Most hotels and resorts at Thekkady, Kumily, Vandanmedu and Pirmed can arrange visits to plantations.*

Temples

There are a number of temples near Periyar Tiger Reserve. One of the best known is Mangaladevi Temple, situated on the crest of a hill, but it is now largely neglected and is only open for certain festivals. Permission is required from the forest department office at Thekkady to visit this temple.
Wildlife Preservation Officer, Periyar Tiger Reserve, PO Kumily, Thekkady. Tel: 0486 922 2027.

Elephants roam freely around Periyar National Park

MUNNAR
Munnar town

At 1,652m (5,420ft), Munnar has developed into a hill resort for visitors to Kerala. It is a small town with a spectacular setting near Annamudi, South India's highest peak. The abbreviation of two Tamil words, *moonu* (three) and *aar* (river), Munnar lies at the confluence of the Kuthirappuzh, Nallathanni and Kundala rivers.

Like other hill stations of India, the small town of Munnar was discovered and established by the British to serve the needs of some of the world's highest tea plantations. Until the late 19th century, Munnar was a deeply forested area inhabited mainly by tribal groups like the Madhuvans.

The growth of Munnar as the commercial centre of tea estates began in 1887 with the opening of the High Ranges of Travancore, also called the Kannan Devan Hills, for agriculture. An official of Travancore, Munro, was the first to lease the hill tracts for agriculture. After experimenting with rubber, chichona and other crops, the planters found the area suitable for the cultivation of tea. The giant tea company of James Finlay & Co was established in 1895 and eventually controlled most of the tea estates around Munnar. Access to Munnar was by train from Tamil Nadu until 1931 when a road was opened from Kochi, making life easier for the planters.

In 1964, the Finlay estates went into a joint venture with the Tatas, one of India's wealthiest families. Today, Tata Tea controls most of the tea production around Munnar and is among the largest producers in India. The tea from their Kannan Devan Estate is especially famous.

Munnar still has colonial buildings, including old bungalows, and recreational life is focused around the clubs which were set up for British planters.

Munnar is 304km (190 miles) from Thiruvananthapuram, 153km (96 miles) from Kochi and 287km (179 miles) from Kozhikode.

Christ Church

This Protestant church, built in 1910, is set on a hill near the town centre. It has a pleasant interior which is notable for its stained-glass windows, and its original pews can still be seen. The cemetery on the hillside above the church is older, with tombs dating from 1894 and brass plaques in honour of the planters.

This church is in Old Munnar and has services in Tamil and Malayalam. The Christmas Mass is popular.

Tata Tea Museum

Old equipment and photographs documenting the tea-making process are on show at this museum. Thirsty visitors can also take part in some tasting.

1.5km (1 mile) north of town centre. Tel: 0486 523 0561. Open: 10am–4pm. Admission charge.

Munnar environs

Devikulam

Devikulam has beautiful views over the high ranges of the Western Ghats. Devikulam Lake is in a private estate and you will need permission from the Tata office at Munnar to visit it.

The lake is particularly beautiful, and locals believe that Sita bathed at the lake, and so they consider it to be holy and possess curative powers. The name Devikulam means 'the lake of the goddess'.

15km (9 miles) from Munnar town.

Kerala

Packing up the tea for processing at Munnar

Tour: Munnar to Top Station

Most visitors to Munnar come to explore the surrounding hills with their neatly manicured tea estates and forests. One of the prettiest routes is the drive from Munnar to Top Station, with its high-altitude tea estates, as well as flowering plants such as Neelukurunji, an orchid that blooms every 12 years, covering the mountain sides with colour.

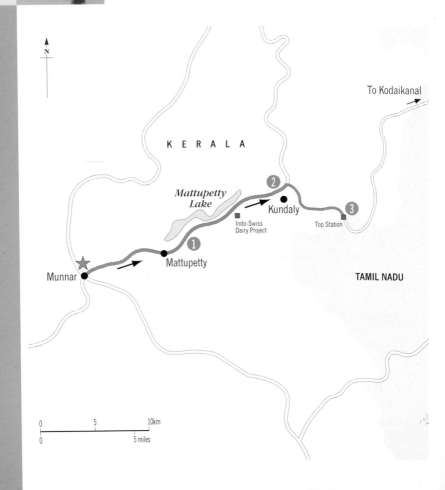

To Kodaikanal

KERALA

Mattupetty Lake

Kundaly

Indo-Swiss Dairy Project

Top Station

Mattupetty

Munnar

TAMIL NADU

0   5   10km

0   5 miles

Although the distance from Munnar to Top Station is only about 34km (21 miles), you need to allow 4–5 hours for the return trip, as the mountain roads are slow-going. It is also a good idea to check on the road conditions before setting off: during the rainy season fallen trees are not uncommon.

Take the road from Munnar to Top Station, leading past tea estates, some of which have retail outlets. It may be possible to obtain permission to visit one of the tea estates and see a working factory. Plantation activities such as tea picking can be seen from the road on working days.

The lush landscape near Munnar

1 Mattupetty Lake

At an altitude of 1,700m (5,577ft), this huge lake was created by a hydroelectric project. It has been developed as a tourist attraction, and facilities include speedboat rides and horse riding. Elephants and wild boar are sometimes seen in the surrounding forests.

3km (2 miles) after Mattupetty, you will see the entrance of the Indo-Swiss dairy project, which is now run by the Kerala Livestock Development Board as a cattle breeding and research centre. From here the road rises to Kundaly.

2 Kundaly

The dam at Kundaly is a few hundred metres off the road. Full of trout and other fish, it has a beautiful setting in the hills and is surrounded by grasslands and forests, where elephant and gaur (Indian bison) can sometimes be spotted. An old colonial inspection bungalow stands in the woods near the lakeshores. Four kilometres (2¹/₂ miles) from the dam is a golf course, with an attractive clubhouse, administered by Tata Tea for planters and guests. Permission is required for a visit or a game and the last stretch of road requires a jeep.

After Kundaly, the road ascends to Top Station.

3 Top Station

At 2,200m (7,218ft), Top Station, on the border of Tamil Nadu, has a great view of some of India's highest tea plantations. Little now remains of the ropeway that was used to transport tea to the valley floor, called Lower Station.

From Top Station you can return to Munnar. Some travellers may wish to use this route to travel on to Kodaikanal, a hill station in Tamil Nadu.

Tour: Wildlife trail from Munnar to Chinnar

The 60km (37-mile) route from Munnar to Chinnar Wildlife Sanctuary, at the Tamil Nadu border, is great for seeing a variety of endangered flora and fauna from the sandalwood tree to the Nilgiri tahr.

This is a full-day tour and an early start is necessary as the roads are hilly, and some walking is involved at Rajmalai, Marayoor and Chinnar.

Take the road north from Munnar to Rajmalai, and turn left from the main road about 14km (9 miles) from Munnar.

1 Rajmalai

Rajmalai has the only permissible path for visitors in the **Eravikulam National Park**, home of the endangered Nilgiri tahr. A relative of the domestic goat, the Nilgiri tahr has erect ears, long sturdy limbs and rounded horns that end in an impressive curving sweep. It does not have the beard and twisted horns of a goat, but it is just as agile and sure-footed.

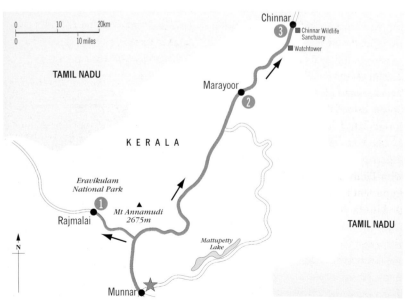

Designated a national park in 1978, Eravikulam was previously set up as a sanctuary for the protection of the Nilgiri tahr. Spanning an area of 97sq km (37sq miles) of *shola* habitat, comprising rolling grassland and forest, the park contains the high peak of Mt Annamudi (2675m/8776ft). Besides Nilgiri tahr, Eravikulam is also the home of elephant, tiger, panther, wild dog, Nilgiri langur, lion-tailed macaque and giant squirrel. From the gate of Rajmalai, the steep path leads to the Tata Tea Estate, which affords good opportunities to see the Nilgiri tahr and a variety of birds.

Eravikulam National Park. Tel: 0486 523 1587. www.eravikulam.org; roywlw@eravikulam.org.
Open: Sept–May daily 7am–6pm.
Admission charge.
Return to the highway and drive north past tea estates and a Hindu shrine. To the left of the highway is Marayoor village.

2 Marayoor

This natural sandalwood forest is the only substantial one left in Kerala, and it is strictly protected. Only dead and diseased trees are removed. The forest officer may be able to arrange treks with Tamil tribal guides. Marayoor has important megalithic sites and prehistoric rock paintings, but be warned that the trek to this particular site is strenuous.

www.marayoor.com.
From Marayoor, the road continues 20km (12 miles) to Chinnar Wildlife

Sanctuary. Langur, bonnet macaque and peafowl are often seen from the road. Just off the main road is a watchtower, which is great for viewing wildlife.

3 Chinnar

Chinnar was declared a wildlife sanctuary in 1984 and contains a range of habitats from *shola* forest and grasslands in the hills to drier forests in the rain shadow region. This 90sq km (35sq mile) reserve has elephant, gaur, deer and panther, as well as the rare grizzled giant squirrel which is hard to spot. A good variety of birds and butterflies can be seen along the path to the watchtower.

Chinnar Wildlife Sanctuary. Tel: 0486 523 1587; enpmunnar@sify.com.
Open: daily 7am–6pm. Admission charge. The drive from the entrance of Chinnar Wildlife Sanctuary direct to Munnar is 52km (32 miles), but expect to spend 3–4 hours on the road.

A Nilgiri tahr in Eravikulam National Park

KOZHIKODE
Kozhikode city

Kozhikode, or Calicut, is one of the cities most associated with the spice trade. Mentioned in the writings of Marco Polo, Kozhikode was ruled by a dynasty with the title Zamorin, which means 'king of the seas'. The Zamorin had strong alliances with the Arabs, giving them a monopoly over the spice trade.

The Zamorins were also patrons of the arts and of culture in general, and Kozhikode became famous for its textiles (calico is said to derive from Calicut, the colonial name of the city). In the 15th century, the power of the Zamorins covered about half of Kerala.

The balance of fortunes between the Zamorin and other rulers of Kerala changed when Vasco da Gama discovered an alternative route to Kerala from Europe which broke the Arab monopoly over trade westward from India. Vasco da Gama's fleet is said to have landed at Kappad near Kozhikode in 1498. Unsuccessful in forging links with the Zamorin, he turned his attention to Kochi. Seeing the alliance between the Dutch and the Kochi Raja as a threat to their trade monopoly, the Zamorin set out to conquer Kochi, but the Portuguese intervened and made Kochi their protectorate. The Zamorins survived two Portuguese attacks, although one severely damaged Kozhikode, and they eventually made peace with the Portuguese in order to remain

contenders in the spice market. Sultan Hyder Ali conquered Kozhikode from the Zamorin, and his son Tipu ruled it for some time. Later, the British vanquished the Sultans and took control of Malabar, making it a province of their Madras Presidency in 1800.

Kozhikode was a centre for rebellions against British rule, beginning when the British administration made laws that supported the landlords rather than the farmers. The Indian National Congress found enthusiastic support in the Malabar province, and the death of prisoners being transported in a railway carriage triggered a rebellion in 1921.

Today, Kozhikode is a commercial centre of Kerala's northern districts and an important centre for the timber trade and for boat building. Known for its old Moplah and Nair houses, Kozhikode has also experienced much new building activity in recent years.

Kozhikode is 382km (237 miles) from Thiruvananthapuram and 188km (117 miles) from Kochi, with good road and rail connections. It also has an international airport.

Mananchira

Little remains of the Zamorin's old royal enclave at Mananchira. Locals believe the Zamorin killed himself in his palace, rather than face defeat at the hands of the Mysorian Sultans after peace talks failed. Temples, mosques and churches surround the square.

Mosques

The Kuttichara area of Kozhikode is known for its medieval mosques. The four-storey **Mishkal Mosque** is in the traditional Kerala style, with gabled roof and wooden columns; partly burned by the Portuguese in 1510, most of the original building still stands. Another mosque in the traditional style is the **Muccunti Palli,** which has a slab stating that the land was a donation from the Zamorin.

The mosques are within walking distance of each other.

Museums

The **Pazhassiraja Museum** has interesting models of different kinds of megalithic monuments of Kerala and replicas of Hindu temples, as well as collections of coins, bronzes and copies of original murals. Next door, the **Krishna Menon Museum** (*Tel: 0495 238 1253*) has clothes, speeches and photographs of this former defence minister of India, while the Art Gallery in the same building has an excellent collection of paintings by Indian artists, including Raja Varma.

The museums are on East Hill about 5km (3 miles) from the city centre. Museums open: 10am–12.30pm & 2.30–5.00pm. Closed: Mon and Wed morning. Free admission.

Tali Temple

This temple is known for its woodcarvings and huge statues of the

Muslim women and children wait at a bus stop in Kozhikode

deities. Probably dating from the reign of the Zamorin, it is now an important religious centre in Kozhikode.
The temple is south of the city centre. Open to Hindus only.

Kozhikode environs
Beypore

Beypore has been a shipbuilding centre for many centuries. Today, its yards produce hand-built dhows called *urus*, which are exported to the Gulf countries. Visitors can buy miniature replicas. Beypore is also known for its Tasara Creative Weaving Centre which trains artisans in textile skills.
8km (5 miles) south of Kozhikode.

Kadalundi Bird Sanctuary

This bird sanctuary at the estuary of the Kadalundi River has a number of resident species of kingfishers, herons and gulls. It is best visited in winter when flocks of migrants come here.
The sanctuary is on two sides of the river 19km (12 miles) south of Kozhikode.

Kappad

Kappad has a stone memorial marking the spot where Vasco da Gama is said to have landed in 1498. The beach at Kappad is popular with day trippers from Kozhikode, as the city's own beaches are rather crowded.
About 16km (10 miles) north of Kozhikode.

Kottakal

Kottakal is home to the Arya Vaidya Sala Hospital, which is regarded as one of India's most renowned Ayurvedic centres, and which has been

Wind-drying a saree on Kappad Beach

The Vasco da Gama memorial pillar at Kappad

involved in research and practice for more than 100 years.

48km (30 miles) south of Kozhikode. Arya Vaidya Sala, Kottakal. Tel: 0483 274 2216. www.aryavaidyasala.com; mail@aryavaidyasala.com

Mahe

Mahe has an interesting colonial history, first under the British and then as a French colony under Pondicherry. The French arrived at Malabar in the 17th century to establish its spice-trading base. Located on a hill and overlooking a river, the town was named after Mahé de Labourdonnais who conquered it in 1725. Handed over to the Government of India in 1958, Mahe has few remnants of its French colonial history, one exception being **St**

Theresa's Church (*Tel: 0490 233 2332*). The town also has an arts institution, the **Malayala Kalagramam Centre for Arts and Ideas**, which offers courses in music, dance, sculpture and painting.

60km (37 miles) from Kozhikode towards Kannur. For information about courses contact Malayala Kala. Tel: 0490 233 2961.

Vadakara

The **Lokarnarkavu Temple Complex** (*Tel: 9960 696 620*) is 5km (3 miles) from the town centre of Vadakara. It has three temples, with the oldest and biggest dedicated to Durga and the others to Vishnu and Shiva, as well as a number of rock caves and tanks. The temples have attractive carvings near the entrance and some interesting paintings inside.

Vadakara is on National Highway 17.

KANNUR
Kannur city

Kannur, or Cannanore, was an important spice-trading port, visited by the likes of Marco Polo. Ruled for centuries by the Kolatri Rajas, European powers began to exert their influence from the 15th century. The Portuguese made it a military base, building a fort which took advantage of Kannur's position on raised ground above cliffs facing the sea.

After a period of Dutch rule, Kannur became an important British centre in 1790. Besides the buildings erected by the Europeans, it also has some old quarters of the local Moplah (Mapilla) Muslim trading community.

Kannur is 278km (173 miles) northwest of Kochi, 90km (56 miles) northwest of Kozhikode and 465km (289 miles) northwest of Thiruvananthapuram, with good rail connections to these cities, and to Mumbai, Delhi and other major Indian cities.

The impressive St Angelo Fort was built by the Portuguese at the turn of the 16th century

Beaches

Kannur has a number of beaches, although none of them is particularly well known as a tourist destination. The most popular is Payyambalam Beach, near the fort.

St Angelo Fort

This fort was built by the Portuguese in 1505 during the Viceregalship of Almeida. The Dutch occupied the fort in 1663 and sold it in 1772 to the Ali Raja of Kannur, who was the first Muslim ruler of Kerala. Ali Raja had a short tenure, before the British conquest of 1790 made St Angelo Fort one of the most important British army bases in South India. Built from laterite blocks, the fort walls are protected by the sea, and by a moat on the landward side. The British practically rebuilt the rest of the fort within the walls for their garrisons, and some of the old cannons still stand, but the highlight of a visit to the fort is the view of the sea, and occasionally of the fishing fleet returning with their catch.
Open: daily 9am–6pm.
Free admission.

Kannur environs
Chirakkal

This was the capital of the Kolatri Rajas when they ruled Kannur, and the wooden mansion that served as their palace can be seen here. Chirakkal also has some interesting temples.
6km (4 miles) from Kannur.

Parassinikadavu Temple, near Kannur

Parassinikadavu Temple

This temple rises on the banks of the Valapatanam and is associated with the legend of Muthapan, the hunter form of Lord Shiva, who is said to have appeared before (or been born to) a Shiva-worshipping childless landlord couple. As a hunter, Muthapan did not appeal to the landlord family, so Shiva appeared before them in his divine form. He was fond of toddy, and was given it whenever he was called upon to perform a miracle, which is why toddy remains the main offering at the temple.

The non-conformist temple has always been open to all castes, and to non-Hindus as well. The main tourist attraction is to attend the dawn and dusk Teyyam performance which opens and closes the temple ceremonies. The Teyyam here portrays the legend of Muthapan, said to have selected Parsinidakavu as his sacred home. Muthapan is depicted with a dog as a companion, and therefore street dogs are welcomed and offered toddy and fish.

The temple is about 18km (11 miles) from Kannur. Teyyam *is performed daily at 6.30am & 5.45pm. Donation appreciated.*

Thoddikulam Temple

This temple, east of Kannur off the road from Thalasseri to Mananthvadi, is known for its murals, believed to date from the 16th century.

The temple is about 25km (16 miles) east of Thalasseri (see pp76–7).

Cottage industries

Called the 'Land of Loom and Lore', Kannur is known for its handloom weaving industry that is said to date back to the 16th century. The success story of its handloom exports over the last 50 years or so has earned it recognition from the Government of India as a 'Town of Export Excellence', and a planned textile park near Kannur is set to open during 2008 to make the most of its expertise. From traditional sarees and sarongs, the weaving units and handloom cooperatives have now diversified into home furnishings for the export market. About 100,000 people in Kannur district are employed by the textile sector.

It is possible to view the entire process from spinning to weaving, to dyeing – just ask permission in the office. The Kanjirode Handloom Weaver's Cooperative Society is one of the oldest, established in 1952, and it turns out cotton and silk fabrics, soft furnishings, sarees and *dhotis* (sarongs). In 2002, it set up a common facility centre for other units in the district that lacked dyeing equipment and other infrastructure, making this one of the best places to see the many stages of Kannur's

Deft finger work is required in the workers' cooperatives

textile industry. The cooperative has many different kinds of loom, including a 2.3m (91-inch) Malabar loom. Many of the cooperatives also have retail centres where visitors can buy shirts, fabrics and furnishings.

At the Kerala Dinesh Beedi Workers' Cooperative near Kannur you can see workers making *beedis*, the local cigarettes that are popular in India. Owned and managed by the workers and retirees, most of them women, the government supports the cooperative's aims, which are to improve the income of *beedi* workers and to give them better working conditions than elsewhere. Most of the workers are 'rollers', who cut the leaves before filling them with tobacco and rolling them into reefers. The *beedis* are then tied into bundles and sent to the packing and shipping departments.

An important feature of the unit, embodying the literacy and political awareness of the people of Kerala, is the 'reader' who reads aloud from the local newspapers so that the workers can hear. There are also meals and washroom facilities, and workers are entitled to leave allowance, gratuities and a retirement pension. The purchasing, marketing and financial accounting departments are centralised for all the production units in the cooperative. Although the cooperative has been successful in

Selling garlands in Thiruvananthapuram

improving the conditions of Kerala's *beedi* workers and has sustained profitability for most of the years of operation, it has fallen on somewhat harder times since smoking has been banned in a number of public places.

The cooperative has worked on other projects such as agro-processing, making and packaging curry powders, pickles, coconut cream, jams and other popular food products. There has also been a move into information technology, which has established data-entry training centres and entire software business parks with development centres, networks, computer labs and design centres, a library, and internet and counselling facilities. However, the income has not been enough to sustain employment. In 2006, the government gave the cooperative a grant of 40 million Rupees to assist workers' families and help the enterprise diversify.

Tour: Kannur to Thalasseri

This 22km (14-mile) tour covers the attractions on National Highway 17 between Kannur and Thalasseri, known for their forts.

Allow about 4–5 hours for the return trip.

Take National Highway 17 south from Kannur to Thalasseri. After 8km (5 miles) you will come to Muzhappilangad Beach.

1 Muzhappilangad Beach

This is one of the finest beaches in Kerala, stretching for 4km (2¹/2 miles) along a bay with a wide strip of white sand. The palm trees to the north and the rocks to the south make it ideal for photographs of 'picture-postcard' sunsets. However, the Muzhappilangad is being promoted as a 'drive-on' beach

Bulls at the roadside near Kannur

by the tourist authorities, and so it can get very crowded during holidays. *Continue on National Highway 17 for about 3km (2 miles) to Illikunnu, just off the highway.*

2 Illikunnu

German missionary Herman Gundert settled at Illikunnu in 1889 and stayed for about three decades. It was here that he wrote the first Malayalam journal and the first Malayalam–English dictionary. The house is in typical Keralan style but is closed for public viewing.
Return from the house to the highway and drive to Thalasseri.

3 Thalasseri

Thalasseri, or Tellichery, was one of the most important British military bases in Malabar, and it was the site of their first factory in Malabar. The British obtained permission from the Raja of Chirakal to build the fort at Thalasseri in order to protect their interests in spices along the coast and in the hill plantations. The fort was built in 1708 and successfully withstood the struggle between the British and the Mysorian sultans. Entered by an impressive gate flanked by comical images of guards, the fort has high walls and an abandoned lighthouse, and there are many tales of the secret underground tunnels leading from the fort. Behind it are other colonial buildings, including two churches and a school. The cemetery contains the grave of Edward Brennan,

who was the founder of Brennan College, a highly respected institution.

Thalasseri also has old Moplah houses of the Muslim merchant families. Their mosque is in traditional Malabari style, and local accounts say it dates to the 16th century. Thalasseri is also known for its gymnastics school, run by the national sports authority, and for its kalari centre, which instructs students in the traditional martial arts of Kerala. *It is a 11km (7-mile) drive from Thalasseri back to Kannur.*

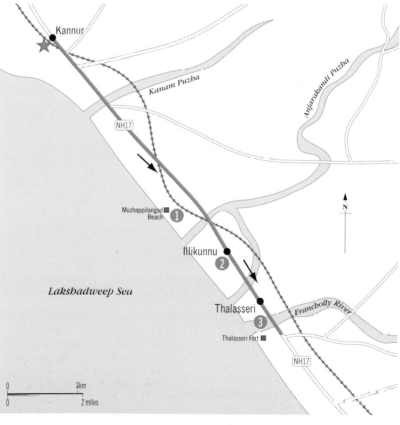

KASARAGODE
Kasaragode city

The name of the northernmost district of Kerala derives its name from the Sanskrit for 'land of lakes'. Ruled by the Nayakas, Kasaragode town fell to Tipu Sultan and came under British rule after the Mysore Wars. It now has a large Muslim population and is known for its mosques, but also has many interesting temples and lovely beaches, so it is being developed into a tourist centre.

Kasaragode is 344km (214 miles) from Kochi, 156km (97 miles) from Kozhikode and 560km (348 miles) from Thiruvananthapuram, with good train connections.

Mosques

With a large Muslim population, the town has many mosques, including the beautiful **Malik Deenar Jumma Masjid**, built in Keralan style. This mosque is believed to be the burial site of Malik Ibn Dinar.

Kasaragode environs
Anantha Padmanabha Temple

This temple is believed to date from the 9th century, although the present structure is more recent, and it is venerated as the original abode of Padmanabhaswamy, the deity of Thiruvananthapuram. Set in a small lake, the temple has a bridge connecting the *gopuram*, or gatehouse, and the sanctuary. The principal deity, Vishnu, is shown sitting on the serpent Anantha, and not reclining as in the more famous Padmanabhaswamy Temple at Thiruvananthapuram. The murals depicting Puranic themes have been recently restored to their former glory. *The temple is east of Kasaragode town. Open to Hindus only.*

Bekal

Bekal is famous for its fort, which offers superb views of the sea. Originally said to be part of the Kadamba kingdom,

---

PUPPETRY IN KERALA

Yakshagana Bombeyatta is a form of puppetry that now, sadly, has few practitioners, although some can still be seen in Kasaragode. It is based on the Yakshagana folk theatre of Karnataka, and uses song and elaborately costumed puppets to relate tales from the Hindu epics. String puppets and rod puppets are used, and their costumes and movements enact the role of the character in the story. Sri Gopalakrishna Yakshagana Bombeyatta Sanga at Kasaragode is an organisation promoting and performing this folk art.

Puppetry also survives as a performing art form in Palakad district, and the village of Partithupuli is home to the Adi Pandaram puppeteers who came to Kerala from Andhra Pradesh. Despite its origins in Telugu, the language of Andhra Pradesh, this form of glove puppetry is influenced by Pavakathali, the Kathakali dance drama. Pavakathali employs painted puppets decorated with peacock feathers to portray scenes from the *Mahabharata* and other epics.

Tolpava Koothu, literally 'leather puppet play', enacts tales from the Ramayana by projecting shadows of leather puppets onto a white background. This is a ritualised folk art performed on a stage facing the deity, Kali, and 100 or so puppets can be used in a single performance.

Bekal passed on to the Vijayanagara dynasty and the Kolatri Rajas. The fort was probably built in the 17th century when the Nayakas took Bekal after the decline of Vijayanagara. Tipu Sultan took Bekal, and the British occupied the fort after they defeated the sultan. The walls of the fort are still intact, and a tunnel leads from the interior directly to the sea.

Dedicated to Hanuman, Anjaneya Temple is built against the fort walls, while south of the fort is Bekal Beach. Six kilometres (4 miles) from the fort is another good beach, at Kappil.

The fort is 80km (50 miles) northeast of Kannur. Tel: 0467 227 2900. Open: daily 9am–5pm. Nominal admission fee and a video camera charge.

Chandgiri Fort

This is one of a string of fortresses built along the coast by the Nayakas in the 17th century. Though largely neglected, Chandgiri Fort is worth visiting for its good sea views.

3km (2 miles) south of Kasaragode.

Kottancherry

Kottancherry is a pleasant place for walks in the Western Ghats.

30km (19 miles) north of Konnakkad.

Nileshwar

Nileshwar is known for its government-approved yoga institute.

Nileshwar is south of Kasaragode past Bekal towards Kannur.

The Malik Deenar Jumma Masjid (mosque), said to be the burial site of Malik Ibn Dinar

Kerala

WAYANAD

Wayanad is one of the most forested districts of Kerala, and it has a high tribal population. The district is also known for its waterfalls and wildlife. The name, Wayanad, is believed to be a shortened version of the word *Valnadu*, meaning 'land of paddy', and the local economy thrives on rice fields, tea, coffee and spice plantations.

The headquarters of Wayanad district is Kalpetta, 251km (156 miles) from Kochi, 63km (39 miles) from Kozhikode and 467km (290 miles) from Thiruvananthapuram.

Edakkal

The **Edakkal Caves** comprise Kerala's most famous prehistoric site, featuring petroglyphs sculpted into the rocks. The drawings are formed by geometric lines and are generally dated to about 10,000 BC. Some scripts are said to be dated from the 3rd century BC. There are also good views of the surrounding hills.

Ancient tombstones in the Manantwadi churchyard

12km (7¹⁄₂ miles) from Sultan's Bathery. Tel: 0493 622 1860. www.edakkal.com; info@edakkal.com. Open: daily 8.30am–4.30pm. Admission charge.

Heritage Museum

This museum exhibits archaeological finds from the district, mainly 14th- to 16th-century sculptures of deities, as well as tribal artefacts such as local jewellery, weapons and fish traps, and agricultural implements.

Ambalavayal, 25km (15¹⁄₂ miles) from Kalpetta. Open: daily 10am–5pm. Admission charge.

Manantwadi

Manantwadi has a 19th-century church that serves the Christian converts among the local tribal population, especially the Kuruchiyas. The churchyard has some old tombstones.

Manantwadi is 32km (20 miles) north of Kalpetta.

Plantations

Wayanad has a number of tea, coffee and spice plantations. The district is also one of the highest producers of arecanuts (beetlenuts).

Hotels and resorts at Vythri and Kalpetta arrange plantation visits.

Pookot

Pookot has a lake that has been developed for recreational tourism with boating facilities. Opposite the lake is **Narayana Guru Ashram**.

63km (39 miles) from Kozhikode.

Sultan's Bathery

This town is named after Tipu Sultan, but there are few signs of the sultan's fort which the British destroyed. There is a **Jain temple** in the town which probably dates from the 12th or 13th century, and which has carved ceilings. *98km (61 miles) northeast of Kozhikode. Regular buses from Mysore, Kalpetta and Kozhikode. Sultan's Bathery has hotels and restaurants.*

Thirunelly

Thirunelly has an important Vishnu Temple, sometimes called 'the Kashi of Kerala'. Devotees bathe in a mountain stream called Papanasini, which they believe brings visitors eternal bliss. *North of Kalpetta via Manantwadi.*

Wildlife reserves

Wayanad Wildlife Sanctuary forms part of the **Nilgiri Biosphere Reserve**. Access is from Tholpetty near Manantwadi in the north, or from Muthunga near Sultan's Bathery in the south. Across the border in Karnataka, **Nagarhole** or **Rajiv Gandhi National Park** can be accessed from Karapur near Manantwadi and **Bandipur National Park** by continuing on the road past the Muthunga entrance. You are likely to see elephants, sambar, spotted and barking deer, gaur or Indian bison, wild boar, hanuman langur and bonnet macaque. Fortunate visitors could spot sloth bear, but tiger, panther and dhole (wild dog) sightings are rare. Mastigudi in Nagarhole is a

The Jain temple at Sultan's Bathery

good place to see large herds of elephant during the dry months. These forests are also rich in birdlife, including grey jungle fowl, red spurfowl, Malabar pied hornbill, hill mynah, crested serpent eagle, hawk eagle and many other colourful species. Wetland birds can be seen along the Kabini River.

A permit for the Wayanad sanctuaries can be obtained from Muthunga or Tholpetty. Admission, vehicle entry, guide and camera charges are paid to the local forest officer. There are usually jeeps standing near the forest department offices for hire to visit the sanctuary. Nagarhole. Tel: 0821 248 0901. Open: daily 6–8am & 3–5.30pm. Admission charge. Bandipur National Park. Open: daily 6.30–9am & 3.30–5.30pm (approx.). Admission charge.

Karnataka

Karnataka is perhaps the most diverse of the four states of Southern India. It has varied scenery, from the long coastline and forested hills to the ancient rocky outcrops of the Deccan Plateau, as well as a rich architectural legacy of 5th- to 12th-century temples, medieval mosques, the eclectic palaces of Mysore, and numerous forts. Its cultural diversity encompasses the tribal villages in the hills, and the traditional temple towns, as well as the modern, cosmopolitan atmosphere of Bangalore, making it a richly rewarding destination for travellers.

The coast of Karnataka has many fine beaches and mangrove estuaries, while the hills are among the wettest areas of the Western Ghats. Here you will find spectacular waterfalls, along with the headwaters of great rivers such as the Krishna, the Kaveri (also spelt Cauvery) and the Tungabhadra, as well as forests rich in wildlife. Much of the state falls in the Deccan, and is home to some of the world's oldest granite and other ancient rock formations.

For most travellers, it is the state's historical legacies that are of special interest. The Hoysalas took advantage of turbulence in Southern India to establish a strong kingdom from the 11th to the 14th centuries in the southern part of the state. Their magnificent temples, at Belur, Halebid and around Mysore, testify to the Hoysala wealth and might: these temples are built on distinctive star-shaped platforms, with an ambulatory around the main building, which has splendidly carved exteriors and ornate columns in the interiors.

Islamic incursions into Karnataka began in the 13th century, and the Brahmani Sultanates became prominent in the northern areas of the state, such as at Bidar, between 1422 and 1526. The Vijayanagara kingdoms united against the Islamic invasions and founded their capital at Hampi in 1336. Hampi remained an important seat of power for two centuries and has a splendid selection of both sacred and royal monuments.

Temples were central to the urban life of Vijayanagara, and their main architectural features include the large temple complexes, with towering gatehouses, or *gopurams*, at cardinal points, and walls enclosing purpose-built structures to make the temples focal points for meetings, education, dance, theatre and wedding ceremonies. They introduced columned *mandapas* for ceremonies and subsidiary shrines for the consort of the presiding deity, with the wedding anniversary often being celebrated in the temple.

As Vijayanagara declined, the Islamic Sultanates dominated Karnataka, founding great monuments at Bijapur, Bidar and Gulbarga, including walled citadels, mosques, mausoleum complexes and tanks in a restrained Turkish style but incorporating the rich craftsmanship of the local artisans.

When the Sultanates began to decline in the face of Mughal and British conquests, the Wodeyars established their rule from Mysore. After losing to Hyder Ali and his son, Tipu Sultan, the Wodeyars were reinstated by the British after they took the forts of Tipu Sultan, and they became one of the two most affluent and influential rulers of India, with majestic palaces at Mysore.

After independence, the Maharaja of Mysore handed over his princely holdings and Mysore became a state of India in 1950. Over recent decades, the Kannadiga (Kannada-speaking) areas of the Madras Presidency and Hyderabad princely state, and the region of Coorg (Kodagu), were united to form the state of Karnataka.

Karnataka

Carved pillar, Hampi

BANGALORE
Bangalore city

The capital of Karnataka, Bangalore is known for its strong export and hi-tech industries, making it the capital of India's information technology revolution. Bangalore's strong manufacturing base includes electronics, aeronautics, machinery and export-quality fashion garments.

While the first impression that most visitors get of Bangalore is of bustling modernity, its tree-lined avenues also justify its title of Garden City, while various monuments testify to a vibrant history.

Bangalore was founded in the 16th century by Kempe Gowda, changing hands frequently. From the mid-18th century, the city was ruled by Hyder Ali, who is credited with the Lalbagh Gardens, which were further developed by his son and successor, Tipu Sultan, who both extended Bangalore and built a wall around it.

After the British overthrew Tipu Sultan in 1799, the city began to take on the ordered look of a colonial town over the following century.

Bangalore's airport receives international and domestic flights. It is connected by rail or air to most of the other important cities of Southern India.

Bangalore Palace

This replica of England's Windsor Castle dates from the 1880s and was subsequently sold to the Wodeyar rajas of Mysore, whose descendants still live in it. Ownership is currently being contested, and it is not open to the public.
Palace Road.

Bull Temple

One of the earliest monuments of Bangalore, dating from the reign of Kempe Gowda, the Bull Temple is named after the huge monolithic Nandi, the bull of Lord Shiva, which is carved out of stone and decorated with bells.
Basavanagudi. Open: daily 8am–8pm. Free admission.

Cubbon Park

Besides being a welcome green space and having a sports complex, Cubbon Park is of interest to travellers because of its museums. The **Government Museum** here is one of the oldest in Southern India, dating from the 1880s, and it has Neolithic and Harappan relics, fine Hoysala, Chalukya and Chola sculptures, jewellery, textiles, coins, miniature paintings of the Deccani and other schools, and geological exhibits. The **Venkatappa Art Gallery** exhibits the paintings and sculpture of the 20th-century artist after whom it is named, as well as other permanent and temporary exhibitions. The **Visvesvaraya Industrial and Technological Museum** has a good transport collection and informative sections for children.
City Centre. Government Museum/ Venkatappa Art Gallery.
Tel: 0802 286 4483. Open: Tue–Sun 10am–5pm. Nominal admission charge

(same ticket valid for both).
Visvesvaraya Industrial and
Technological Museum.
Tel: 0802 286 4009. Open: daily 10am–
5.30pm. Admission charge.

Iskcon Temple

This temple was built by the International Society for Krishna Consciousness from 1990 to 1997, blending the traditional architectural style of Karnataka with modern innovation.
Harikrishna Hill, west of Chord Road.
Tel: 0802 347 1956. Open: daily
sunrise–sunset.

Lalbagh Botanical Gardens

Lalbagh was laid out in the mid-1700s by Sultan Hyder Ali and his son, Tipu, who were inspired by the Mughal Gardens of Northern India and the French gardens of colonies like Pondicherry. Some of the original trees that were planted by the Sultans, as well as by the British who brought in

gardeners from Kew, still stand. Besides the exotic plants and trees that can be seen along the pathway, notable features of Lalbagh are the Rose Garden, the Floral Clock and the Glasshouse, which was inspired by London's Crystal Palace and holds flower shows on Republic Day (26 January) and Independence Day (15 August).
South of the city centre.
Tel: 0802 657 3667. Open: sunrise to
sunset. Nominal admission charge.

Vidhan Soudha

One of India's most attractive state secretariat buildings, Vidhan Soudha was built in the 1950s and has an impressive granite façade with carved ledges, huge columns and a dome crowned by the national emblem. Nearby are a number of colonial buildings, including the High Court of Karnataka.
Northern edge of Cubbon Park. Closed to
the public.

Karnataka

Iskcon Temple

Walk: Bangalore's historic centre

When Kempe Gowda founded Bangalore – then named Bengaluru, 'city of boiled beans', because it is said that in 1537 he was offered beans by an old woman – he built a mud fort at the site and mapped out the potential extent with four watchtowers at each corner. While Bangalore's urban sprawl has far exceeded his expectations, the fort still stands. This walk explores the old city centre of Bangalore that was founded by Kempe Gowda and later developed during the reign of Tipu Sultan.

Allow 3 hours to see the monuments.

Start from Tipu Sultan's Palace. The walk covers a short but congested stretch of road.

1 Tipu Sultan's Palace

This palace was started by Sultan Hyder Ali and extended in the 1780s and 1790s by his son, Tipu, who made it his summer palace. Built along the lines of their Daria Daulat Bagh at Srirangapatnam (*pp90–91*), Tipu Sultan called it *Rashk-e-Jannat*, the abode of happiness, envy of heaven. Though it is no longer in the best of conditions, it is still a hauntingly atmospheric place and has a well-kept garden, wooden walls and ceilings with murals in brilliant colours, cusped arches and teakwood columns with elephant-headed cornices, European-style bases and capitals in brilliant colours. The palace was converted by the British into the commission's office in Bangalore and now houses a picture gallery.
Palace open: daily 9am–5pm.
Admission charge.
Turn right out of the palace to visit the neighbouring Venkataramanaswamy Temple.

2 Venkataramanaswamy Temple

This temple, built in the Dravidian style with towering *gopuram* gateways, pyramidal towering roof and lavishly carved columns, is reputed to be 300 years old, but it was in fact rebuilt by the Wodeyars, probably sometime during the 18th century.
Open: daily 8.30am–6pm. Closed every other Sat.
At the junction outside the temple, turn left on Krishna Rajendra Road for the Bangalore fort.

3 Bangalore Fort

This 16th-century fort, originally built out of mud by Kempe Gowda, was subsequently fortified by Hyder Ali with

stone walls and a moat. The fort today is rather dilapidated and some of the walls have been damaged, but the impressive granite gateway and the walls which bear inscriptions give an indication of the military traditions of the period. Inside are dungeons, cells and passages.
Bangalore Fort. Tel: 0802 336 0818.
Open: Mon–Sat 10am–6pm.
Admission charge.
Return to the road and continue to the City Market.

4 City Market

This crowded market is one of the busiest places in Bangalore and has a congested bus station. The bazaars, selling all manner of spices, fruits, vegetables and other commodities, are dominated by the impressive domes and minarets of the surrounding mosques.
Open: daily 5am–10pm.
From City Market, retrace your steps to Tipu Sultan's Palace.

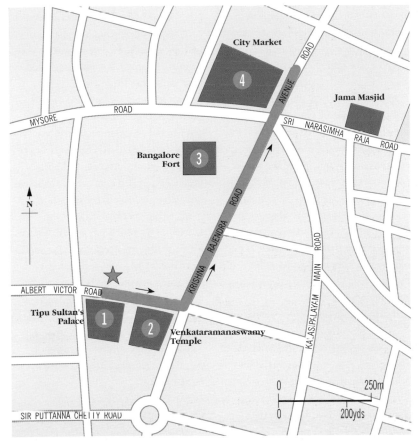

MYSORE
Mysore city

Known for its palaces, flower markets, silk textiles and sandalwood factory, Mysore takes its name from the demon, Mahisura, who is said to have been slain on Chamundi Hill overlooking the city by the goddess Chamundi.

The Hoysala dynasty ruled this region and built an impressive temple at Somnathpur nearby. The Vijayanagara dynasty ruled much of Karnataka until they were overthrown by the Islamic invasions of their capital, Hampi, in the 1560s, at which time the Wodeyars carved out an independent kingdom. They held sway over the state, except for a brief period when Hyder Ali and his successor, Tipu Sultan, took over the reigns until the British took control. During the British reign, Mysore prospered and the Maharajas (rulers) introduced wide-ranging reforms and civil improvements. Second only to the Nizams of Hyderabad in precedence among the princely states of India, the Maharajas of Mysore built flamboyant palaces and lived a life punctuated by elaborate processions and ceremonies. They had stables full of elephants and horses, and garages full of Rolls-Royces and other expensive cars, as well as their own silver railway carriages.

At the time of independence, Maharaja Jayachamarajendra Wodeyar of Mysore agreed to the accession of his princely state to India and was appointed governor of the new state of Mysore.
Mysore is about three hours from Bangalore by train or road.

Chamundi Hill

This hill is topped by a temple to Chamundeshwari, who is said to have destroyed Mahisura at this site, and who was a patron deity.

City Palace

One of the largest palaces in India, Mysore's City Palace was built in 1912 on the site of an earlier wooden palace that was destroyed by fire. The architect, Henry Irwin, blended Hindu, Islamic and European styles. The car passage, complete with cannons and carriages, leads to the doll's pavilion with its sculptures, ceremonial objects, wooden elephant howdah decorated with gold, and antique dolls. The Kalyan Mandap, or wedding hall, has murals recording Dussera and other ceremonial processions, together with gold-painted cast-iron pillars rising to a stained-glass dome painted with peacocks and floral patterns, a massive brass chandelier and mosaic floors.

A marble staircase leads to the Durbar Hall, which has a marble floor inlaid with semi-precious stones and paintings by some of India's most renowned artists. The private hall has gold-leaf work on the columns, ivory-inlaid doors, and fine woodwork on the ceiling. A museum in the palace complex exhibits Mysore paintings and relics of Karnataka's princely past.
Mirza Road. Tel: 0821 243 4425.
Open: daily 10am–5.30pm.
Admission charge.

Jagan Mohan Palace

This palace, built in 1861, was converted by HH Sir Jaya Chama Rajendra into an art gallery in 1955. The galleries display decorative arts, with fine collections of porcelain, glassware and ivory artefacts, as well as portraits of the Mysore royals and British dignitaries, oil paintings and watercolours by Indian artists from the early and mid-20th century, musical instruments and other exhibits.

At the western end of the City Palace. Tel: 0821 242 3693. Open: daily 10am–5.30pm. Admission charge.

Railway Museum

Among its collection, this museum has a vintage steam-driven fire engine, a 1914 MG car that could run on rails, a 1922 narrow-gauge train, a 1920 E-class engine and a 1910 Lever Frame inspection car. Of particular interest is the Sri Ranga Pavilion, which houses an 1899 saloon carriage and its accompanying dining car that once belonged to the Maharaja of Mysore.

Krishnaraja Sagar Road. Open: Tue–Sun 10am–1pm & 3–5pm. Admission charge.

Mysore's ornate City Palace

Tour: Around Mysore

Mysore makes a good base for a tour of sites of both historic and natural importance. This tour takes in one of Karnataka's most popular bird sanctuaries, one of India's best-known gardens and one of Karnataka's most important forts. Taxis can be hired in Mysore for the tour.

Allow about 6 hours, including sightseeing time.

Take the Bangalore highway to Srirangapatnam, about 12km (7½ miles) north of Mysore.

1 Srirangapatnam

Occupying an island site on the Kaveri, Srirangapatnam is named after the Sri Rangananatha Temple, built by a governor of the Ganga kingdom in the 9th century, which also served as a refuge for Ramanuja, a religious reformer of the 12th century. Over the years the site played a significant role in the political development of Karnataka, until it was eclipsed by Mysore and Bangalore. The fort was built in the 15th century by the Vijayanagara rulers, and after their decline it became part of the Wodeyar kingdom. The fort became the headquarters of Hyder Ali, when he ousted the Wodeyars from the area, and it has close associations with Tipu Sultan, who made it his headquarters and developed the area by introducing agricultural reforms. He was killed in the battle of Srirangapatnam, a battle that helped the future Duke of Wellington (Colonel Arthur Wellesley) make his military reputation, and the fort subsequently became a British headquarters with Wellesley as the governor.

Srirangapatnam contains the ruins of the triple-walled fort, including gates, ramparts, dungeons, and cemeteries with British and French gravestones. There are Hindu temples in the complex, as well as the mosque of Tipu Sultan with its delicately decorated slender minarets and inscriptions.

About 1km (½ mile) east of the fort complex is Daria Daulat Bagh, the Garden of the Wealth of the Seas, with its formal gardens surrounding a palace made of teak in an Indo-Saracenic style. The palace has large murals recording the life of Tipu Sultan, especially battle scenes, ornamental arches, gilded paintings and floral decorations on its wooden walls and ceilings, while a museum upstairs exhibits coins, European paintings, manuscripts, engravings and the sultan's belongings. *Head west for Ranganathittu Bird Sanctuary, about 3km (2 miles) upstream from Srirangapatnam.*

2 Ranganathittu Bird Sanctuary

One of the country's oldest-protected bird areas, this river site was established by the Maharaja of Mysore at the suggestion of India's well-known ornithologist, Salin Ali, who realised that a weir created by the Wodeyars in the 17th century had created a reservoir that was an important habitat for waterfowl. Today, it is protected by the government as a bird sanctuary. Boats can be hired at a jetty for a tour of the islands, where there are many opportunities for getting remarkably close views of spectacular congregations of many species, including storks, egrets, ibises, cormorants, herons and plovers, which all breed here. Crocodiles often bask on the islands, and some visitors have also seen mongooses, bonnet monkeys and monitor lizards along the shores. Large roosts of flying foxes and other bats are also seen in the sanctuary.

Drive north to Brindavan Gardens, a short distance from the Bird Sanctuary. Open: daily 8.30am–6pm. Admission charge.

3 Brindavan Gardens

These gardens are situated by the side of a reservoir named after Maharaja Krishnaraj Wodeyar, who built a rock dam to provide water for the nearby power station. Large crowds come to see the fountains and the gardens which are usually illuminated after sunset, making an attractive sight.

Open: daily 7am–8pm. Admission charge. From the gardens, it is a 19km (12-mile) drive southwards to Mysore.

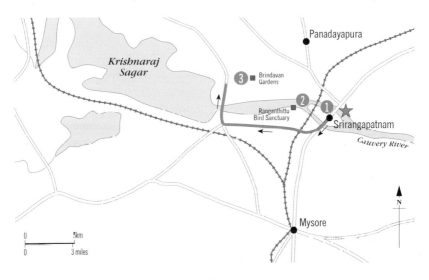

BELUR AND HALEBID

The Hoysala dynasty, who ruled southern Karnataka from the 11th to the 13th centuries, built great temples at Belur and Halebid in the 12th centuries. The distinctive feature of these temples is that they look modest and squat from a distance but are in fact carved in great detail, with hardly any area of the surface left without ornamentation.

The temples are built out of soft soapstone, making it possible to create deep relief carvings. The star-shaped plan is followed by the base and the shrine, with the high plinth providing a circumambulatory walk for pilgrims. Inside the temples are lathe-turned pillars that resemble the rounded wooden columns found elsewhere, while a bell-shaped tower and exquisite carvings are some of the highlights, blending the Dravidian and northern Nagara styles of architecture. The sculpture is magnificently detailed.

Hassan is the nearest railway station to Halebid and Belur. There are hotels in and around Hassan.

Belur

Once the capital of the Hoysala kingdom, Belur is home to the 12th-century **Chennakesava Temple** (*Open: sunrise–sunset. Free admission*), which was built by King Vishnuvardhana. The temple – which is still very much in use – is set in a courtyard, along with a number of smaller shrines, and its exterior displays some exquisite

sculptures of female figures, bands of elephants, musicians, dancers and deities, and perforated screens carved with tales from the *Puranas*. Inside, the Narsimha column has astonishing detail, while the sanctum contains a sculpture of Krishna with his consorts.

Halebid

The **Hoysaleshwara Temple** at Halebid (*Open: sunrise–sunset. Free admission*) is the largest of the Hoysala temples, even though it is unfinished. It has the usual star-shaped plinth, complete with bands of elephants, lions and horsemen, floral scrolls and outstanding narrative friezes with scenes from the Hindu epics. The temple is carved with fine images of Brahma on his swan, Krishna playing a flute, and Ravana trying to shake Mount Kailasha, the abode of Lord Shiva. The lawns of the temple are very attractive and house a museum of sculptures.

A short distance from the Hoysala temple, some Jain shrines exhibit lathe-turned columns.

Sravanabelagola

Most visitors to the temples of Halebid and Belur also visit Sravanabelagola to see the colossal statue of Gomateshwara that is sacred to Jains. One of India's largest freestanding sculptures, the 10th-century statue, about 17m (56ft) high, is reached by a flight of about 700 steps after a strenuous climb. The nude statue has elongated arms and wide shoulders that are somewhat out of proportion, but the hands, hair and serene face are perfectly carved.

The statue tells of Bahubali, who defeated his elder brother Bharat over a right of succession, but, after winning the battle, realised its futility and adopted a life of meditation and asceticism. The depth of his meditation is depicted with creeper growing on his limbs and ant hills and snakes at his feet.

The ascent to the statue leads past Jain shrines, most of them dating from the 12th century, and some have very fine carvings. There are also Jain temples in the town and on nearby Chandragiri Hill.

Chennakesava Temple in Belur

KODAGU

With its forests, waterfalls and plantations, Kodagu district, often called the Coorg region, is one of the most scenically attractive areas of Karnataka. Once ruled by regional kings, the Haleri rajas, Kodagu has a distinct cultural identity that differs from that of the rest of Karnataka, with its own cuisine, language and costumes, along with a strong pride in its martial tradition.

Markets called *shantes* are held weekly and can be experienced on Fridays at Madikeri and on Tuesdays at Kushalnagar. Among the many attractions of the area are Sidhapur, which is one of the major coffee-growing areas, the Dubare forests and elephant camp, and Kakkabe, which makes a good starting point for climbing Thandiandamole, at 1,750m (5,741ft) the highest peak in the region. The island of Nisargadhama, on the River Kaveri near Kushalnagar, is a good spot for birdwatching, among a pleasant setting of parkland and a variety of trees, including bamboo and sandalwood.

Bylakuppe

A number of Tibetan settlements are scattered around Bylakuppe, which is one of the largest areas of Tibetan Buddhism in Southern India. Here Buddhists have established craft cooperatives as well as schools. One of the most important monasteries here is the *gompa* at Sera which serves as the Mahayana Buddhist University, one of India's foremost learning centres for Tibetan monks or lamas. The most prominent feature of the *gompa* is the massive image of Shakyamuni Buddha. Another of the region's attractions is the Golden Temple of Namdroling, a beautifully painted monastery in peaceful grounds. The prayer hall has enormous gilt statues of Guru Padmasambava, Shakyamuni Buddha and Buddha Amitayus, richly decorated columns with dragon motifs, *thangka* wall paintings, a beautiful casket, and galleries that offer an insight into Tantric Buddhism. Another important monastery in the region is at Tashi Lhumpo.

Bylakuppe and the monasteries can be accessed from the Mysore–Madikeri Highway.

Madikeri

The market town of Madikeri, which is the capital of Kodagu district, spreads along the edges of the hills. The town's main attractions are the 19th-century **Omkareshwar Temple**, which exhibits a fascinating blend of Kerala-style pagoda roofing and façades with Islamic domes. Near the temple is a fort with stone gateways, while **St Mark's Church**, within the fortifications, is now a museum showing British relics, Jain and Hindu sculpture, and regional art and culture. Nearby are the royal cenotaphs and an 18th-century Shiva Temple. **Raja's Seat**, said to have been a royal pavilion, has a superb view of the surrounding hilly countryside.

An uphill road through coffee estates and woods leads to the Abbi Falls which are set among pepper and flowering vines, cardamom plants, bamboos and forested hillsides.

Madikeri is about three hours by road from Mysore.

Omkareshwar Temple. Open: daily 6.30am–noon & 5–8pm

St. Mark's Church Museum. Open: Tue–Sun 10am–5.30pm. Free admission.

Raja's Seat. Open: daily 5.30am–7.30pm.

Talakaveri

Spelt Talacauveri on some maps, this is considered to be a source of the River Kaveri and is therefore a place of pilgrimage for Hindus. In October, during a festival called Kaveri Sankaramana, pilgrims come to bathe in the river and to visit the springs. About 8km (5 miles) away, at Bhagamandala, is the Triveni bathing ghat at the confluence of the Kaveri, Kanike and Suiyorhi rivers. The Bhandeshwara Temple here is a striking Kerala-style building in a large stone courtyard.

48km (30 miles) from Madikeri.

Karnataka

The stunning Kodagu landscape

HISTORIC TOWNS OF NORTHERN KARNATAKA

Northern Karnataka comprises the northern part of the Deccan Plateau, and it is veined by the Tungabhadra, Krishna, Doni and Gataprabha rivers.

One of the area's main attractions is the great temples established by the Chalukya rulers in the 6th and 7th centuries. These include those at the World Heritage Site of Pattadakal, the Vijayanagara temples and courtly architecture of the 14th to 16th centuries at Hampi, which is also a World Heritage Site, and the 15th- to 17th-century mosques and mausoleum complexes of Bijapur and Bidar, which are regarded as some of the best examples of Islamic architecture in Southern India.

Aihole

Generally referred to as the cradle of temple architecture, Aihole has more than 100 temples built in different styles including the early Chalukyan, late Chalukyan, Hoysala, Nagara and Dravidian from the 6th to the 12th centuries. The best known is the Durgigudi or Durga Temple, so-named because of its location near the 'Durg' or fort walls, and noted for its early *gopuram*-style entrance structure, Buddhist-style semicircular apse, and elevated plinths featuring panels of intricate carvings. The gallery around the sanctum displays a series of elaborate sculptures in niches; these include Lord Shiva with Nandi, Narasimha, Lord Vishnu with Garuda, Varaha or the boar incarnation of Lord Vishnu, Durga or Chamundi destroying the buffalo-headed demon Mahisura, and Harihara, the combination of Vishnu and Shiva. Amorous couples are sculpted on the columns, and the entrance doorway to the hall has outstandingly fine sculpture.

46km (29 miles) from Badami.
Durga Temple. Open: daily 8am–6pm.
Admission charge.

Badami

Set among sandstone ridges, Badami was the stronghold of the Chalukya rulers, who excavated caves in the sandstone cliffs around the town and built impressive temples at Aihole and Pattadakal.

Badami has a railway station. There are hotels and places to eat in the town.

Badami cave temples

The caves cut into the sandstone ridges of Badami in the 6th and 7th centuries are said to have influenced the design of structural temples built later on in the Deccan. The three Hindu and one Jain caves are known for their fine sculptural work, including the minute detail of the jewellery worn by the deities and the smaller figures. Cave 3, which is dedicated to Vishnu, is generally considered to be the most impressive of the four cave temples, not only because of its elaborate sculptural decoration but also because of its sheer size. The cave has striking depictions of couples as carved brackets, Lord Vishnu on the

coils of the serpent Anantha, and Vishnu's incarnations as Narasimha, the man-lion combination that disembowelled a demon, and Varah or the boar incarnation. The sculpted columns and fine images of Indra on an elephant, Shiva on a bull and Brahma riding a swan on the ceiling panels are among the most detailed in Badami.
Open: daily sunrise–sunset.
Admission charge.

Bidar

At the centre of Bidar is the medieval walled town of the Sultans, with its many mosques, a great 15th-century *madrasa* or theological college with a towering minaret and fine mosaics, and a fort built by the Chalukyas and strengthened during the reign of the Sultans after Ahmed Shah made the town his capital in the 15th century. The fort contains the remains of palaces, such as the Rangin Mahal, with its fine woodcarvings and inlay work. Ashtur, east of Bidar, has some impressive domed mausoleums of the Sultans.
137km (85 miles) from Hyderabad.

Bijapur

Bijapur's building boom came in the 16th and 17th centuries after the five Islamic rulers of the Deccan joined forces to invade the Vijayanagara capital of Hampi.

The town's largest and most celebrated monument, the **Golgumbaz**, was built as the mausoleum of Muhammad Adil Shah in the 17th century. The hallway of the main mausoleum is one of the largest in the world to be covered by a single hemispherical dome, which also dominates the townscape. The **Ibrahim**

Golgumbaz mausoleum, Bijapur

Rauza, one of the highlights of Bijapuri architecture, was built by Ibrahim II, who came to the throne in the 1580s, and his wife, Taj Sultana. The mausoleum has minarets, cupolas, stone filigree, fine sculptural work, pierced windows and decorative panels. It also exhibits elaborate Koranic inscriptions that rank among the best in India.

Bijapur's Juma Masjid, or **Jami Masjid**, dating from the 16th century, is one of the Deccan's finest mosques. Superbly proportioned and topped by onion domes, the mosque has an arcaded court with a square tank. The court leads to the main prayer hall, with its elegant central dome surrounded by 33 smaller domes. The *mihrab* or prayer niche is richly embellished with gold work, calligraphy and floral decorations.

Bijapur has a railway station and a few hotels. Golgumbaz. Tel: 0835 225 0725. Open: daily 6am–6pm. Admission charge. Ibrahim Rauza. Open: daily 6am–6pm. Admission charge. Jami Masjid. Open: daily 9am–5.30pm.

Hampi

Hampi epitomises the grandeur of the great Vijayanagara Empire, which is regarded as the largest Hindu empire of Southern India. The town is home to clusters of ruined monuments, called the **Royal Centre** and the **Sacred Centre**, and scores of temples and other buildings set among the hills and along the Tungabhadra River. The most glorious period of Hampi was during the reign of Krishnadevraya, who saw the Vijayanagara Empire grow in power, wealth and extent. Great patrons of art, the Vijayanagara rulers also worked towards the development of agriculture, textiles and new technologies.

Hampi is near Hospet, a town with a railway station and a few hotels.

Royal Centre

The best representation of the courtly style of the Vijayanagara dynasty, which drew on both Hindu and Islamic architectural styles, is the 16th-century **Lotus Mahal**, screened by a wall as it was probably built for the queens (some believe it was a council as the elephant stables are nearby), with cusped arches, bracketed windows and pyramidal domes. The **elephant stables** have ten domed chambers, with vaulted entrances representing different architectural styles, and beams to which elephants could be chained, around a central pavilion, with a guardhouse at the entrance.

The hydraulic engineering skills of the Vijayanagara rulers can be seen in the tanks, ducts, canals and sluices that carried water to different areas of the Royal Centre.

3km (2 miles) south of Hampi. Lotus Mahal & elephant stables. Open: daily 8am–6pm. Admission charge.

Sacred Centre

Some of the temples of Hampi predate the Vijayanagara kingdom. The oldest is probably the **Virupaksha Temple**, still in use today, which has *gopuram* gatehouses added by the Vijayanagara rulers, as well as some of the few remaining examples of the Vijayanagara style of painting. A short walk from the Virupaksha Temple, the **Vithala Temple** is considered to be one of the finest examples of Vijayanagara architecture. Believed to date from the 16th century, the temple contains the famous 'Hampi chariot', a shrine designed in the shape of a wooden chariot on wheels, with fine carvings including a depiction of Garuda, the eagle mount of Lord Vishnu. The open *mandapa* or hallway features intricate carvings, while the slender, superbly carved columns produce musical notes when struck. The ceiling is beautifully carved with floral and geometric patterns. The other columned halls also have interesting carvings.

Virupaksha Temple. Open: daily 6am–8pm (closes for 2 hours around noon). Vithala Temple. Open: daily 8am–6pm.

Pattadakal

Once the site of coronation ceremonies of the Chalukyan rulers, Pattadakal's temples date from the 3rd to the 7th centuries and are considered to represent the most mature phase of Western Chalukya architecture. Some of the temples were built by the Rashtrakutas after they took over the kingdom from the Chalukya dynasty. The best known are the **Malikarjuna** and **Virupaksha** temples, which were built for two sisters, who were queens of the Chalukyan ruler, Vikramaditya. They have richly carved three-storey

towers, with striking panels showing different forms of Shiva and Vishnu, and a carved base. Like most of the temples of Southern India, the interiors are also exquisitely carved, with the pillars of the Virupaksha Temple relating tales from the *Ramayana* and *Mahabharata* epics, while those of the Malikarjuna Temple are carved in delicately executed relief and depict scenes from the life of Krishna. Other carvings in the temples reflect the courtly and social life of the Chalukyas.
17km (10½ miles) from Aihole. Temples. Open: daily 6am–6pm. Admission charge.

Virupaksha Temple, Hampi

Tamil Nadu

Tamil Nadu occupies the southeastern corner of India running down to the tip of the peninsula at Kanyakumari. The state has a handful of quite distinctive regions – the Nilgiri hills, or the Western Ghats, that reach altitudes of 2,500m (8,200ft), the fertile Kaveri River basin, the arid and semi-arid regions inland, and a long coastline with fine beaches, saltwater lagoons such as Pulicat, estuaries and the Gulf of Mannar.

The forests of the Nilgiri hills are rich in wildlife, especially elephants and birdlife, while the Gulf of Mannar and the wetlands near the coast are good sites for watching waterfowl and wading birds.

But for most visitors to Tamil Nadu, the highlights are the Dravida Temples that run along the coast. The development of the Dravida style of architecture began during the reign of the Pallava dynasty who built the *rathas* or chariot-like monolithic shrines at Mahabalipuram. These shrines were a step up from the cave temples of the past, as they involved creating roofs and columns, and subsequently incorporated the standing structure of the Mahabalipuram shore temple in the 7th to 8th centuries. The temple architecture of the Pallavas reached its zenith at Kanchipuram.

The Cholas, who took control of the Kaveri basin from the 9th to the 12th centuries, built temples with tall pyramidal towers on high bases and introduced recessed bays, cells and niches with carved images. The Pandiyas, who succeeded the Cholas, built temples in concentric walls, which were often fortified, with huge *gopuram* gatehouses; examples can be seen at Tiruchirappalli, Chidambaram, Tirumalai and Darasuram.

After Islamic invasions of Southern India, the Vijayanagara kings united to form a strong kingdom in the Deccan and influenced Dravida temple architecture from the 14th to the 16th centuries by making enlarged complexes with purpose-built areas including columned marriage *mandapa* halls. They also introduced more subsidiary shrines for the consort of the presiding deity and other associated deities and figures, and *gopurams* at cardinal points.

In the 17th century, the Nayakas emerged as a power in Southern India with their capital at Madurai. They built temples with dominating *gopurams* covered with rich decorations and long colonnaded halls. Temple tanks were a major feature of these temples, and the Nandi bull stood in most Shiva shrines.

The European colonial powers also left a rich architectural legacy in Tamil Nadu, and in the town of Pondicherry Union Territory along the coast. The British buildings of Chennai, such as Fort St George, Egmore Station, the High Court, and administrative buildings and churches, are among the most impressive colonial structures in Southern India, while the French built churches in Pondicherry, as well as a number of public buildings and houses. These can be seen while walking along the promenade or roaming the streets, which still show their French names on signboards.

Tamil Nadu's impressive temple architecture and colonial buildings, together with its vibrant, living tradition of language, literature, customs, music and dance, and its natural diversity of landscapes and wildlife, make this a fascinating place to visit.

In contrast to the traditional temple towns and the tribal villages of the hills are the industrial centres of Tamil Nadu, with the capital, Chennai, being one of the four largest cities of India.

Tamil Nadu

Rural life in Tamil Nadu

CHENNAI
Chennai city

Chennai, or Madras, is the capital of Tamil Nadu, and it is often considered to be the gateway to Southern India as it has the largest international airport among the four states. One of the four metropolises of India, it is also an important port and industrial centre.

The city is a relatively modern one, established by the British in the 17th century, but incorporating ancient sites and old Portuguese villages. Because the British stayed here longer than in other cities of Southern India, Chennai has some of India's earliest and most impressive examples of colonial architecture.

330km (205 miles) east of Bangalore, Chennai has an international airport.

Churches

It is believed that Thomas the Apostle arrived in Kerala and took refuge in the Little Mount Caves south of Chennai. The **Basilica of San Thome** is one of the city's famous churches; it was probably founded in the 16th century, and is situated in an area that used to be a Portuguese enclave. The present cathedral dates from the 1890s, and was built in the Gothic style. St Thomas Mount in the cantonment is associated with the last years of St Thomas, and it has a 16th-century church.

Basilica. Tel: 0442 498 5455. www.santhomechurch.com. Open: daily 4.30am–9pm. Free admission.

Egmore

Egmore is home to some of Chennai's best-known colonial buildings, including **St Andrew's Kirk**, built in the 1820s. This church is a fine example of the architecture of this period, with its towering steeple, columned nave and huge dome, painted with stars on a blue background and supported by Corinthian columns. The Egmore Railway Station and the municipal buildings and colleges are other important colonial structures in the area.

St Andrew's Kirk, Poonamallee High Rd. Tel: 0446 453 3694. Open: daily 8am–6pm. Admission free.

Government Museum

This museum is one of the best and most comprehensive in Southern India. Established in the mid-19th century, the museum is a red circular building with Mughal influences and European columns housing a museum and a theatre, as well as the **National Art Gallery**, which was designed by Henry Irwin in the early 20th century and is situated in the same compound. The museum's collections include tools, jewellery and weapons from the Stone and Iron ages, as well as geological exhibits. One of the most important collections is of sculpture, especially those found at Amrawati and other Buddhist sites of Andhra, such as Nagarjunakonda and Goli. The collection includes relief panels telling the life of Buddha, images of the *Jataka* tales, a votive slab from the Amrawati *stupa*, and statues of Buddha, standing with a serene and meditative face. There are also impressive stone sculptures from Tamil Nadu and Karnataka which represent Pallava, Chola, Hoysala and Chalukyan art.

The museum is also well known for its bronze gallery. Its superb collection of 9th- to 13th-century metal sculpture, ranging from about 4cm (1½ in) to over 1m (3ft) tall, is significant, as Tamil Nadu was known for its bronze-casting industry. The collections include numerous Chola sculptures of Natraja, which symbolise the motion and power of Shiva's cosmic dance in detail,

Somaskadas showing seated Shiva and Parvati with or without Skanda their son, Shiva in meditation sculptured in great detail, Ardhanaishvara, and the renowned figures of the *Ramayana* from Thanjavur.

The ethnology gallery has clothes, weapons and photographs of tribal groups, and a remarkable collection of musical instruments. Numbers two and five of the six buildings that comprise the museum are currently closed for lengthy renovation.

Government Museum, 406 Pantheon Rd, Egmore. Tel: 0442 819 3238.
www.chennaimuseum.org.
Open: Sat–Thur 9.30am–5pm (last admission 4.30pm). Admission charge.

The blinding-white San Thome Basilica

Walk: Fort George

Fort George was founded by Francis Day on land leased from the Raja. It marks the foundation of Madras, today's Chennai. Constructed in the mid-17th century, much of the fort today consists of more recent structures, built after damage incurred from French and other attacks. The thick walls still stand and there are interesting colonial structures in and around the fort. Some of Chennai's grandest colonial buildings can be seen in this area, and in the George Town area nearby.

Allow 3 hours to see the fort and its neighbouring buildings.

Start at St Mary's Church.

1 St Mary's Church

St Mary's Church (*Tel: 044 2567 0389. Admission charge*) is one of the oldest Anglican churches in Asia. It was built in the 1680s and renovated in the 18th century. With its thick walls and strong roof to withstand cannonballs, the church was used as a storehouse and safe refuge during sieges. The interiors are filled with plaques, paintings and statues, many of them depicting key figures in the history of British India, including the former governor of Chennai, Elihu Yale, after whom the famous university is named.

Robert Clive – Clive of India – married his wife Margaret here, and Job Charnock, founder of Kolkata, is believed to have had his daughters baptised here. The church also has some interesting tombstones.

A short walk from the church is the Fort Museum.

2 Fort Museum

The Fort Museum (*Tel: 044 2567 0389. Open: Sat–Thur 10am–5pm. Admission charge*) is situated next to the imposing 18th-century Fort House, which was the main bank and exchange during the colonial period. The museum narrates the history of the British occupation of Chennai, with palanquins, padlocks, flags, weapons, East India Company coins, medals and stamps, as well as uniforms, letters and reports. The art gallery here has portraits and sketches. *From the Fort Museum, continue along the busy main road to the High Court.*

3 The High Court

This judicial building is a splendid example of the kind of Indo-Saracenic architecture promoted by architects such as Henry Irwin. It is a magnificent red building with bulbous white domes, sandstone minarets and spires, and a tall central tower that is a prominent landmark of the city. The interiors of the High Court are equally attractive, with a profusion of stained glass, woodwork, silver panels and ceiling paintings. Nearby is the equally opulent Law College campus, with elaborate twin towers.

Tel: 0442 534 0410.
www.hcmadras.tn.nic.in; hcourt@ tn.nic.in. Open: Mon–Sat 10am–5pm. Free admission; nominal charge for a guided tour.

From the judicial complex it is possible to cross to the grid of streets of George Town. This area has historic temples such as Chennakesavara and Chennamallikesvara, an Armenian Church, an Indo-Saracenic building that now houses the State Bank of India, the robust red General Post Office (ask for GPO), which was designed by Robert Chisholm and completed in the 1880s, and Bentinck's Building, built in Regency style. However, do bear in mind that this is a chaotic, congested and rather unkempt area.

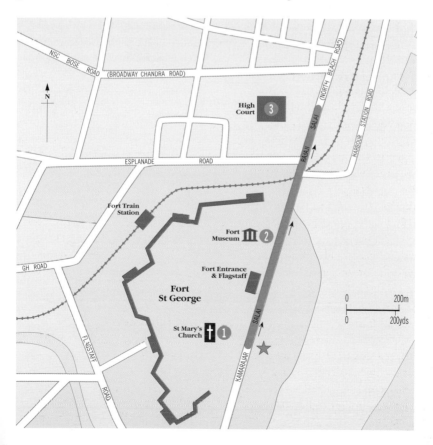

Tour: Artists' villages

The East Coast road from Chennai to Mahabalipuram (Mamallapuram) passes some of the most important arts and crafts complexes in Tamil Nadu.

From Chennai to Mahabalipuram is 58km (36 miles). Allow around three hours.

Take the road 18km (11 miles) south from central Chennai to Injambalkkan to see the Cholamandal Artists' Village.

1 Cholamandal Artists' Village

Established in 1966 to promote the development of contemporary art in India, this village is a place where artists live, work and exhibit their paintings and sculpture. Today, there are many studios and galleries in traditionally designed buildings where paintings, sketches, sculpture, metalwork and other arts are exhibited, and pieces can be bought by visitors. It is sometimes possible to see artists at work in the village or at the galleries.
Tel: 0442 449 0092;
cholamandal@kmronline.com.
About 12km (7½ miles) south of Cholamandal Artists' Village, the highway brings you to Dakshin Chitra.

2 Dakshin Chitra

This heritage centre is one of India's best folk museums, and it encapsulates

the culture and crafts of the four states of Southern India. Set up by a crafts foundation in Chennai, it subsequently received government and international

Stonemason at Dakshin Chitra

information on the traditions of puppetry, dance and tribal cults.

Artisans work on traditional techniques of pottery, basket-weaving, carving, puppet-making, palm leaf decoration and other craftwork. There are also shops and a restaurant.

Music and dance performances are organised here from time to time. *Tel: 0442 747 2603.*
www.dakshinachitra.net.
Admission charge.
From Dakshin Chitra, continue south towards Mahabalipuram. To the north of the village is the Government College of Architecture and Sculpture.

support. In the reception area there is an audiovisual presentation introducing visitors to the concept of the centre and the culture of the states represented. From here, visitors enter an open-air display of domestic architecture from the 19th and 20th centuries, some of which are original buildings that have been relocated to this site. On show are the village huts, houses and workshops of weavers, potters and other artisans, the homes of Tamil Brahmins and merchants, majestic Chettinad mansions containing Chinese crafts and Burmese teak furniture, the wooden Syrian Christian houses of central Kerala, and the Nair mansions of northern Kerala. The complex has successfully re-created an authentic atmosphere of Southern India's dwellings from all four states.

Exhibitions express the cultural diversity of Southern India through textiles such as silk and cotton dresses from a variety of different communities, along with various arts and crafts, and they also provide

3 Government College of Architecture and Sculpture

This is one of the colleges established by the Government of Tamil Nadu to promote sculpture, architecture, music, dance and other traditions of the state. A non-autonomous college under the University of Madras, this can be a good place to gain an insight into the sculptural work of the region, from the preliminary drawings to the execution. The classical tradition of sculpture has strict rules regarding proportion and Hindu iconography. You can get permission to visit from the college office.
From the college, the road continues to Mahabalipuram, with a detour possible to the Tiger Cave, a rock-cut Durga shrine with elaborate lion-head carvings believed to date from the 7th century. With its superb acoustics, the cave may have once been used for performances.

MAHABALIPURAM
Mahabalipuram town

Named after Mahabali, the demon destroyed by Vishnu, Mahabalipuram (also known as Mamallapuram) is one of the greatest draws of Tamil Nadu, with its shore temple and other beautifully sculpted monuments, lively sculptural tradition and travellers' enclave. The variety of fine sculpture seen here has given it the status of an open-air art museum as it shows the progression of Dravida architecture from rock-cut caves through the roofed *ratha* shrines to the shore temple. *Mahabalipuram is 58km (36 miles) south of Chennai.*

Cave temples

The hillside cave temple complex is architecturally interesting as it demonstrates the early Dravida style. One of the most famous caves is the Krishna Mandapa, showing Lord Krishna protecting his people from the wrath of the rain god Indra by lifting Lord Govardhan as an umbrella. Other scenes show Krishna milking a cow and playing a flute. The Ganesh Mandapa is a living shrine and the Trimurthi temple celebrates the trinity of Vishnu, Brahma and Shiva. The Varaha Mandapa has panels showing two reincarnations of Vishnu, Lakshmi and courtly scenes; it also has a water-storage area which is used by pilgrims. The Mahisuramardini Cave is probably the most remarkable, with its carved panel depicting Durga astride a lion

and destroying the demon, Mahisura. The panel also shows Vishnu reclining on his serpent, and statues of Shiva with his consort and his son, Skanda.

An imposing bas-relief near the *mandapas* shows Arjuna, one of the five Pandava brothers, meditating on a nearby statue of Lord Shiva, and a huge elephant leading a procession.

Rathas

The five *rathas* are monolithic, chariot-like shrines sculpted out of rock in the 7th century, each one architecturally distinct. They demonstrate the evolution of temple architecture in Southern India, with *gopuram*, *mandapa* hall and the sanctum, crowned by pyramidal roofs. The tallest of the *rathas* is the pyramidal domed Dharmaraja Ratha, with its row of pavilions and panels of figures dedicated to Lord Shiva, while the largest is the vaulted Bhima which houses an image of Lord Vishnu. The Draupadi Ratha is unique in having a roof resembling that of a thatched house but made of stone. Near the *rathas* stand a sculpted elephant, a lion and a Nandi, the mounts of Indra, Durga and Shiva.

Shore temple

A world heritage site, this shore temple on the coast of the Bay of Bengal is considered by many to be the climax of Pallava architecture at Mahabalipuram. Though eroded by wind, salt and sand, the temple is still remarkable for the extent of the detail that remains even today. The temple is fairly compact, with two finely carved towers, the taller of them standing over a cell facing the sea and showing the introduction of the lion pillar which was the hallmark of this kind of architecture. Built in the 7th to 8th centuries by Rajasimha, the temple is unique in having shrines to both Shiva and Vishnu. It is enclosed by a wall which has panels of animal figures.

Rathas *and Shore temple. Open: daily 6.30am–6pm. Joint admission charge.*

Intricately carved temples, sculpted in the 7th century

Tamil Nadu

KANCHIPURAM
Kanchipuram town

Kanchipuram was the capital of the Pallavas and flourished after their decline. Considered a meeting place for the scholars of three great religions, Hinduism, Buddhism and Jainism, Kanchipuram was a major centre of learning, culture and philosophy, associated with leaders like Sankaracharya and Bodhidharma.

It now houses the remains of Pallava, Chola and Vijayanagara architecture, with its magnificent temples embodying the political importance of Kanchipuram as well as the various stages of architecture from the earlier compact form to the taller *gopurams* and enclosures of the 17th-century temples.

Dubbed the 'golden city of a thousand temples', Kanchipuram is one of the seven holy towns of Hinduism and one of the most important Hindu pilgrim centres of Southern India.

Kanchipuram also has a long history as a weaving centre. For over four centuries it has been famous for its silk sarees with their rich gold thread patterns, and it is also gaining fame for its cotton textiles. Weavers can be watched at work at centres in the town.

As Kanchipuram has more than 70 temples, it is best to aim to visit just a handful over a day or two's stay in the town, or on a day excursion.
Kanchipuram is about 76km (47 miles) west of Chennai.

Ekambaranatha Temple

This is one of the largest of the temples in the town, with five enclosures and a multi-pillared hall called the 1,000-columned *mandapa*. Begun by the Pallavas, the temple developed under the Cholas and was enlarged further by the Vijayanagara rulers who built the high *gopuram* and the outer wall in the 16th century. Dedicated to Lord Shiva, the temple has a tank to its west and an earthen lingam to its east. A carved panel tells the tale of its origins.
Puthupalayam Street. Open: daily 6am–12.30pm & 4–8pm. Nominal admission charge. Sanctum closed to non-Hindus.

Kailasanatha Temple

Rated by most visitors as the most beautiful of the town's temples and also thought to be its oldest, this temple was built from sandstone by the Pallavas. The temple is topped by a pyramidal tower and the walls have cell-like shrines, some with frescoes and *Nandis*. The shrines around the sanctum demonstrate the temple's architectural connection to the Rathas of Mahabalipuram, but Kanchipuram's temple is considered to represent the mature phase of Pallava architecture as it has granite foundations and finer carvings than those of Mahabalipuram.
Putleri Street. Open: daily 6am–12.30pm & 4–8.30pm. Free admission.

Vaikuntha Perumal Temple

Also dedicated to Vishnu, this temple is from the 8th century and is a step up from the older Kailasanatha Temple in its workmanship. Bas-relief panels illustrate battles between Pallavas and Chalukyas, as well as other scenes of courtly life. The lofty tower over the sanctum crowns three shrines. The entrance gateway was added by the Vijayanagara rulers

Kamakshi Amman Sannathi Street.
Open: daily 5am–12.30pm & 4–8.30pm.
Free admission.

Varadaraja Temple

This temple, dedicated to Vishnu, is one of the most important religious centres for pilgrims to Kanchipuram. Built in the 11th century but enlarged during the Vijayanagara period, the temple has a superbly carved *mandapa*, one of the most exquisite in Tamil Nadu, and its main shrine is built on an elephant-shaped rock.

3km (2 miles) southeast of town.
Open: daily sunrise–12.30pm &
4pm sunset. Free admission.
Sanctum closed to non-Hindus.

The beautiful sandstone Kailasanatha Temple

PONDICHERRY
Pondicherry town

The capital of the French colonies in India, Pondicherry was ruled by European colonial powers from the 16th century. The French rule was marked by conflicts with the Dutch and the British who captured the colony for short periods. After 1816, the town began to enjoy peace, and in 1954 Pondicherry was handed over to the Government of India and became a union territory with Kariakal further south, Mahe on the Malabar coast and Yanam in Andhra.

The town retains some of its Gallic flavour in its colonial buildings, and in the French houses of the old quarters. Street signs continue to show both the French and the new Indian names, and the uniforms of the traffic police are still French influenced, while French and Indo-French food is still served in some restaurants.

Aurodhan Art Gallery

The Aurodhan Art Gallery showcases the work of contemporary artists. The exhibits show local influences, including those of the ashrams.
33 rue François Martin.
Tel: 0413 222 2795. www.aurodhan.com;
manager@aurodhan.com.
Open: daily 9.30am–8pm. Free admission.

Auroville

The communes of Auroville, inspired by The Mother (an early 20th-century spiritual leader at the Sri Aurobindo Ashram in Pondicherry), were founded in the 1960s. The place is run on alternative sources of energy, and work here includes handicrafts, organic agriculture and educational projects.
6km (4 miles) north of Pondicherry.
www.auroville.org

Churches

The French influence is visible in the various churches built from the 17th to the 19th centuries, among them the **Church of our Lady of Immaculate Conception**, the **Church of Our Lady of Angels** which has an oil painting given to the church by the king, and the huge **Church of the Sacred Heart of Jesus** which is one of the most impressive, with stained glass and Gothic features.

Goubert Salai

The beachside promenade of Pondicherry offers a glimpse of some of the town's colonial architecture. The **Hotel de Ville** now houses government offices, while a memorial honours Indian soldiers who allied with the French. There is also a French-style square, the Raj Niwas, and a number of other buildings that are relics of French colonial rule.

Government Museum

The Pondicherry Museum displays Neolithic and Roman artefacts, and it has a sculpture gallery with Pallava, Chola, Vijayanagara and Buddhist pieces. It also has a French gallery with furniture and artefacts from the colony, as well as art, handicrafts and geology. There is also a good shell collection. *Government Park. Open: 10am–5pm. Closed: Mon. Nominal admission charge.*

Sri Aurobindo Ashram
One of India's best-known ashrams, this one was founded in the 1920s by Bengali guru Aurobindo Ghose and The Mother. It continues to be the centre of the society he founded, and has beautifully kept gardens with cacti, a rockery and a flower garden, as well as a Samadhi (memorial) of Aurobindo and The Mother, which is covered with flowers. The centre has a few shops, and opposite the ashram is an international centre which sometimes has various programmes worth finding out about if you are in the area.
Information Centre, 3 Rangapillai St. Tel: 0413 223 3604. www.sriaurobindoashram.com; bureaucentral@sriaurobindoashram.com. Main building open: Mon–Sat 8am–noon & 2–6pm. Free admission.

Sacred Heart Church, Pondicherry

CENTRAL TAMIL NADU

The heart of Tamil Nadu, mainly comprising the delta of the Kaveri River, is home to some of the state's most famous temples. This was the stronghold of the Cholas from the 9th to the 13th centuries, and most of the temples in this region were built during their reign, but the Nayakas also contributed to the temple architecture of Thanjavur. Touring this area also gives an insight into the arts of the Tamil rulers, from the superb bronzes and paintings of Thanjavur to the songs of Sangam literature that are still enjoyed today.

Chidambaram

According to legend, Chidambaram is said to be the site of the cosmic dance of Shiva as Natraja who defeated a goddess in a dance competition, ending with the dance of bliss. He is revered here as Natraja, the king of dance, at the **Sabhanayaka Natraja Temple**, which was largely built by the Cholas. Entered through massive *gopuram* gateways, the temple has a gold-plated roof and is noted for its sculpted dance figures depicting the movements of the Natya-Shastra. The centrepiece is the sanctum in the inner enclosure, with its famous Natraja bronzes.

Sabhanayaka Temple, Ayikulam Rd.
Open: daily 6am–noon & 4–10.30pm.
Free admission.
Chidambaram is about six hours from Chennai by road or rail.

Kumbakonam

A former capital of the Cholas, this town has a large number of impressive temples, including the 13th-century Sarangapani Temple which is entered through a tall *gopuram* whose central shrine dates from the Chola period. The temple has intricately carved latticed screens. The 17th-century Kumbareswara Temple has a holy lingam, while the Nageshwara Swami Shiva Temple has fine carvings around the main shrine walls, dating from the 9th to the 10th centuries and rated among the finest in Southern India. The town is important to Hindu devotees, who believe that the Mahmakham tank was the site where the drink of immortality flowed out of Shiva's broken pot and was washed away by holy waters. This town also makes a good base to visit Dasasuram's **Airavatesvara Temple**, which was built by the Cholas in the 12th century and has beautiful carvings, and Swamimalai, a bronze-casting centre. *Kumbakonam can be visited en route from Chidambaram to Thanjavur. Temple 4km (2½ miles) west of town. Open: daily 6.30am–8.30pm. Free admission.*

Thanjavur

The **Brihadishwara Temple** of Thanjavur is one of Tamil Nadu's architectural gems. The high *gopurams* are intricately carved but are dwarfed here by the pyramidal dome over the main shrine which soars about 65m

(213ft) over the plinth and is crowned by a carved cupola. Besides the profusion of imposing sculpture along the exteriors, the paintings inside are also noteworthy. The courtyard is lined with passages, including one which has 108 lingams.

The **Palace of the Nayakas of Thanjavur** now houses a museum containing a gallery of Pallava-, Chola-, Pandya- and Nayaka-period stone sculpture, glass paintings, some princely relics including a throne canopy, and an outstanding collection of about 400 bronze sculptures including some of the best Chola bronzes.

Brihadishwara Temple. Open: daily 6am–noon & 4–8pm. Free admission.

Palace of the Nayakas. Open: 9am–7pm. Admission charge.

Thanjavur is connected by train to Chennai. It has hotels and restaurants.

Tiruchirapalli

Also known as Trichy, this busy town is dominated by its rock fort. Its main attraction is the **Ranganathaswamy Temple** at nearby Srirangam, which has exceptionally finely carved *gopis* and pillars dominated by equestrian sculpture.

Ranganathaswamy Temple. Open: daily 6am–1pm & 3–9pm. Free admission (camera charge).

Tiruchirapalli is connected by train to Chennai. It has hotels and restaurants.

Brihadishwara Temple

MADURAI
Madurai town

Madurai's Meenakshi Temple is not only considered to be one of the greatest sights of Southern India, but also one of the most impressive temples in the world. The town was a capital of the Pandyan dynasty until the 10th century, and it grew to become a centre of commercial trade, through the Tamil seaports, with countries as far-flung as China and Italy. Madurai is also known as a seat of Tamil culture, especially Sangam literature. The present temple building is credited to the Nayakas who took Madurai after it fell first to Islamic powers and subsequently to the Vijayanagara empire.

116km (72 miles) south of Tiruchirapalli, Madurai is served by flights and trains from Chennai.

Gandhi Memorial

This memorial museum is housed in a 17th-century palace of the Madurai Nayaka queens, which was converted by the British into an administrative building. The memorial exhibits Mahatma Gandhi's belongings, his bed, a model of his house at Wardha, paintings and photographs showing scenes from his life, and other relics. It also charts the history of colonised India and has a good account of the freedom struggle. In addition, the palace houses a government museum exhibiting bronzes, stone sculpture, Tanjore paintings, and folk art.

Tamukkam Palace. Tel: 0452 253 1060. www.mkgandhi.org; gandhimmm@lycos.com. Open: Thur–Tue 9am–1pm & 2–6.30pm. Free admission (camera charge).

Meenakshi Temple

The highlight of any visit to Madurai is the Sri Meenakshi Sundareshwara Temple, which is one of India's largest temples, both in terms of compound area and in number of shrines in a single enclosure. The four towering *gopurams* at the cardinal points are more than 43m (141ft) high, rising over huge entrances and carved with fine sculptures of deities, human figures and animals. Highlights of the temple include the Ashta Shakti Mandapa, with its sculpted columns depicting various aspects of Shiva and Shakti, and the tank surrounded by Nayaka murals illustrating the miracles of Shiva at Madurai. An 18th-century mural depicts the marriage of Meenakshi to Sundareshwara, while the Ayirakkal Mandapa (literally 1,000-columned hall) has more than 900 exquisite sculpted pillars as well as an art museum containing bronzes, sculptures and various temple artefacts. The Pudu Mandapam outside the east gate also has marvellously carved columns.

The temple is also an important pilgrimage site for Hindus, and, although the main shrine of Meenakshi is closed to non-Hindus, travellers can watch some rituals here.

*Open: daily 6am–12.30pm & 4–9pm.
Free admission (camera charge).*

Thirumalai Nayak Palace

This impressive palace was built during the reign of a famous Nayaka ruler, and at one time it had galleries, two royal apartments, theatre, temples, armoury and gardens. Much of its original structure was used by his descendants to build new palaces, but the hall of audiences, with its huge columns and a large dome, gives a good impression of how magnificent the original palace must have been in the 17th century.
*Open: daily 9am–1pm & 2–5pm.
Admission charge.*

SOUTHERN TAMIL NADU
Chettinad

This region, named after its Chettiar merchant community, has some of the grandest examples of domestic architecture in Tamil Nadu. The mansions of these merchants comprise successive blocks around courtyards, with carved wooden and granite columns, Italian marble floors, and velvety walls with egg and lime finish rising to gilded ceilings.
Some mansions at Karaikudi and Kanadukathan are open to visitors. These villages are on the route from Madurai to Thanjavur.

Kanyakumari

Also spelt Kanniyakumari on some maps, this town is significant as the meeting place of the Arabian Sea, the Bay of Bengal and the Indian Ocean.
Trains from Thiruvananthapuram.

Rameshvaram

This sacred island in the Bay of Bengal is connected to the mainland by a bridge, the longest in Southern India. It is one of the holiest sites of pilgrimage for Hindus, revered as a *dham* or gateway of the Lord, and is associated with the Ramayana.
Trains from Chennai stop at Rameshvaram.

Tamil Nadu

Ornate carving at the Thirumalai Nayak Palace

Andhra Pradesh

The largest of the four states of Southern India, Andhra Pradesh is the land of great empires. Watered by the Godavari and Krishna rivers, the region was much sought-after by rulers.

From 200 BC to AD 200 the Satavahana dynasty ruled over the area, and subsequently the medieval Kakatiyas reigned over the Telugu-speaking areas. The Nizams of Hyderabad, who were the richest rulers of India with the largest princely state at the time of independence in 1947, endowed the state with some of Southern India's most spectacular sites. These include the Buddhist community at Nagarjunakonda, as well as the impressive palaces, Islamic monuments and museums of Hyderabad. Andhra is also home to a great many magnificent forts, including Golconda Fort outside Hyderabad.

The Andhra capital of Hyderabad is still one of India's most important cities, largely by virtue of its recent growth as a hi-tech centre. Its emerging economy has encouraged investment by international banks and multinational corporations, as well as the IT centres of Cyberabad and Hi-Tech City. Already one of the six largest cities of India, the twin city of Hyderabad – Secundrabad

– has an increasing buzz and modern feel around its plush residential localities and commercial centres.

The heart of Telugu culture can be found around the Godavari and Krishna delta regions, which are among the major rice-producing centres of India. These regions are known for their monuments, poets, artists and musicians. The riverbanks are at their greenest along the coast, where the estuaries' mangrove forests are particularly rich in birdlife and marine wildlife.

Also along the coast is the thriving city of Vishakhapatnam, a shipbuilding centre and port with a strong industrial base, but with beaches and hills nearby that provide welcome relief from the bustle of the city.

All this is in stark contrast to the arid and semi-arid Deccan Plateau of northern Andhra, known for its agricultural problems. It is best, therefore, to focus on the route east from Hyderabad to Vishakhapatnam across the Krishna and Godavari rivers.

The Qutb Shahi Tombs, Hyderabad

HYDERABAD
Hyderabad city

One of India's largest cities, Hyderabad is a charming destination with lakes in and around the city, palaces, mosques and other buildings of interest erected during the reign of the Nizams. It also has bustling bazaars and one of Southern India's greatest forts at nearby Golconda. In contrast to the historic buildings of the city is the recently developed Cyberabad, with its Hi-Tech City, which has become the Indian base for many software development companies.

Hyderabad was laid out in 1591 by Sultan Mohamad Quli Shah on a grid pattern near his fortified citadel of Golconda. It became one of India's richest cities, and the grandeur of Hyderabad attracted Aurangzeb to besiege Golconda and take over the city for the Mughal Empire. As the Mughal power declined, the governor, Asaf Jah, began to exercise his independence; in 1724 he started a dynasty known by the honorific title of Nizam. The Nizam became the wealthiest rulers of India, but in 1948 their princely state was merged into India following military action. The last Nizam, Mir Osman Ali, was allowed to keep his treasures and was given a privy purse as compensation.

Nehru Zoological Park

This zoo, one of the largest in the country, is home to some 3,000 animals. Regular lion, tiger, bear and butterfly safaris are a highlight.

Nehru Zoological Park Road, to the south of the city. Tel: 0402 447 7355. Open: Tue–Sun 9am–5pm. Admission charge.

Ramoji Film City

An hour's bus ride to the southeast of the city, this large studio offers a delightfully kitsch tour plus lunch at a five-star hotel.
Tel: 0402 323 5678. www. ramojifilmcity.com. Open: 9am–6pm.

The Salar Jung Museum

The Salar Jungs were hereditary prime ministers in the Hyderabad court from the middle of the 19th century, and their collection, spanning three generations, was arranged by the third Salar Jung, Mir Yousuf Khan, who died in 1949. Great collectors of art and decorative objects, the Salar Jungs procured paintings, carpets, weapons, textiles, glassware, lacquer-work, bronzes, manuscripts and metalware from across India and also much further afield during their trips and through dealers. Some of their personal belongings, including clothes, utensils, books, furniture and photographs, are also exhibited in the museum. Textiles include hand-woven fabrics and *kalamkaris* (narrative paintings on cloth) of the kind still produced in Andhra. The museum also has a gallery devoted to Indian silk, cotton and woollen textiles, rich silver and gold thread brocades, and floral embroidery from Punjab which is called *phulkaris*. The impressive ivory collection includes chess sets, figures, furniture and other objects, all of them finely carved and some painted. The museum's collection of famous 'Bidriware', or ornate metalwork, of the Deccan, which still thrives in Hyderabad, includes hookahs, trays and plates, and there is also a display of swords, daggers and gunpowder boxes with engraving, inlay work and other decorations on the handles or blades. The museum contains some interesting oil paintings by European and Indian artists, as well as miniature paintings representing various phases in Indian art from Jain palm-leaf paintings to Mughal miniatures and the Deccan School.

Salar Jung Marg, on the southern bank of the Musi River. Tel: 0402 452 3211. Open: Sat–Thur 10am–5pm. Admission charge.

The ruined fort at Golconda

Walk: Markets and monuments around Charminar

The old city of Hyderabad was established on the southern bank of the Musi River in a grid pattern, with arched gateways and stone buildings housing shops and living quarters. Under the Nizams, the city expanded northwards, and the British twinned the city with Secunderabad, housing their cantonment (the clock tower here is a prominent landmark, and there are colonial buildings still standing). The most attractive buildings, however, are to be found south of the river. This area is best toured early before the markets get congested.

Allow 3 hours including sightseeing time.

Start at the southern end of the bridge across the Musi River.

1 High Court

Turn right from the bridge to see the High Court rising from the old gardens on the road running along the southern embankment of the Musi.

This was one of the architect Vincent Esch's best works in Hyderabad, with its Mughal façade built from pink granite with carved sandstone panels and columns, and surmounted by domes. Next to it, the college, designed as a school by Esch, incorporates Gothic features and typically Indian pierced screens.

Walk back to the bridge and then take Sardar Patel Road south past the Charkaman, literally 'four arches', to the Charminar, passing a large market on the way.

Bazaars surround Charminar

2 Charminar

Literally 'four minarets', this yellow stucco building has been a showpiece of Hyderabad from the time when it was built by Sultan Mohamad Quli Shah between 1591 and 1612. The four graceful minarets rise 56m (184ft) high, with spiral staircases leading to the upper storeys.

200m (220yds) south of Charminar, turn right for the Mecca Masjid.

3 Mecca Masjid

This mosque was built in the 17th century by the Sultans and was completed by the Mughal emperor Aurangzeb. One of the largest in Southern India, the red bricks over the arch are said to be made from Mecca clay. Next to the courtyard are the tombs of the Nizams.

Follow the road round from Mecca Masjid as it curves around Lad Bazaar, the market for bangles, pearl necklaces and Hyderabad's handicrafts. Southeast of Lad Bazaar, a lane leads to Chowmallah Palace.

4 Chowmallah Palace

Clustered around a quadrangle with a fountain as the centrepiece, the highlight is the elaborately decorated hall of audiences which houses the seat of the Nizam. The palace displays an extensive collection of textiles.

Retrace your steps from Chowmallah Palace to Charminar, and turn back for the bridge.

Walk: Markets and monuments around Charminar

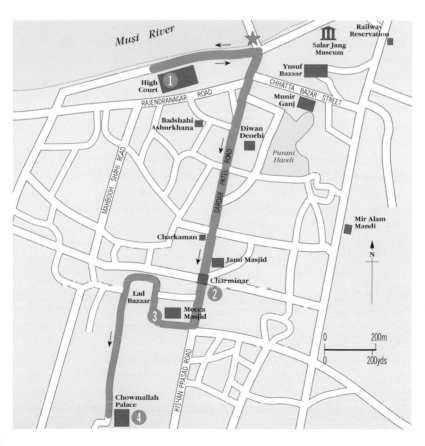

Hyderabad environs

Hyderabad makes a good base from which to visit two of Southern India's greatest forts, Golconda and Warangal. While Golconda is a short drive from Hyderabad, Warangal is a 150km (93-mile) drive or train journey and requires an early start for those who want to return to the city on the same day.

Golconda

The enormous fort of Golconda was founded in the 12th century as the mud fort of the Kakatiyas of Andhra and became the seat of power of the Sultans, who reinforced it with stone walls. After the court moved to Hyderabad, the fort was neglected until it was once again restored by the Nizams in the 18th century. The fort is famous for its three circles of fortifications at different levels, with the main double wall having 87 bastions guarded by cannons and pierced by eight gateways, of which four are in use, housing guardrooms between the outer and inner doorways. Successfully trading in diamonds, pearls and textiles, Golconda grew in importance and the vaults once housed some of the most famous diamonds in the world including, apparently, the Kohinoor. The carved teakwood Fateh Darwaja, the main entrance portico, has superb acoustics that enabled voices, claps, drum beats and bugle calls to be heard all around the fort.

From here the path leads to the beautiful arch of the mortuary bath where dead nobles were bathed before burial, the three-storey armoury and the *zanana* or palace quarters for the harem, where some floral carvings are still visible. Steps lead to the Durbarhall of the Sultans, with its rooftop pavilion overlooking the campus.

The fort was designed to withstand a siege; it has storehouses, water storage and an elaborate hydraulics system of clay pipes and Persian wheels to take water up to the palaces.

About 8km (5 miles) west of Hyderabad. Open: 9am–5pm. Admission charge. Sound and light show every evening; timings vary seasonally.

Qutb Shahi Tombs

The 54m (177ft) high mausoleum of Sultan Mohamad Quli Shah is the most remarkable of about 82 tombs set in and around a garden near Golconda. Collectively the tombs form an attractive site, with their onion-shaped domes, plaster decorations on their granite or green stone walls, and delicate arches.

A visit can be combined with a tour of Golconda. Open: daily 9.30am–5.30pm. Admission charge.

Warangal

The citadel of Warangal was probably laid out during the reign of the Kakatiya rulers of the 12th and 13th centuries. The fort's remains consist of circular fortifications, with a moat around the older outer walls and ornate *torana* gateways that are still imposing. In the centre are the remains of a 12th-century Shiva temple, and an audience hall. The Kakatiyas were great patrons of architecture, and a mature example of the Chalukyan style of temple building can be seen at the temple on Hanamakonda hill, which has Shiva in the sanctum and shrines to Vishnu and the Sun God Surya, as well as beautiful carvings on the doorways, walls and pillars, rock-cut elephants and a large sculpted Nandi.

Warangal can be reached by train from Hyderabad. There are places to stay and eat in the town.

The onion domes of the Qutb Shahi Tombs

NAGARJUNAKONDA

Perhaps Southern India's richest Buddhist site, Nagarjunakonda was a highly cultured civilisation that stretched along the banks of the Krishna River during the reign of the Satavanas and became an important centre of artistic activity under the Ishvaku rulers of the 3rd century AD. It was a planned city, with rampart walls circling it on the three sides that were not protected by the river, and with wide roads, sanitary drainage, public baths and a number of residential areas.

After the Ishvakus were ousted by the Pallavas from Tamil Nadu, the site went into decline, but the opposite bank became the centre of Shiva worship during the reign of the Chalukyas from the 7th to the 12th centuries. The site also saw the development of a fort during the 15th and 16th centuries, when its control was contested between different kingdoms. A Vishnu Temple, five Shaivite temples, and Brahmanical shrines were among the remains found on this side of the Krishna River.

The site was discovered in 1926 in the Nallamalai or black hills beside the River Krishna; here prehistoric and protohistoric remains, Buddhist monuments and other relics had remained undisturbed for some 1,600 years. The original site is now buried under the reservoir created by the Nagarjuna Sagar Dam, but the important remains were relocated and reconstructed on a hilltop that is now an island on the artificial lake.

Nagarjuna Sagar is about four hours' drive southeast of Hyderabad. There are places to stay and eat along the embankment. Launches leave for the island from Vijayapuri, on the banks of the Nagarjuna Sagar daily at 8.30am & 1.30pm.

Anupu

Near the eastern embankments of the Dam, Anupu is the site of the reconstruction of an amphitheatre, which could seat about 1,000 people and had superb acoustics, suggesting an interest in music and performing arts. Some people also believe that this site has connections with Rome. Here you will also find *stupas*, and a *vihara* that is believed to have been a Buddhist university during the 2nd century AD.

Nagarjunakonda Museum

The highlight of the museum on the island site is the 3m (10ft) standing Buddha. Also found here are friezes showing episodes from the life of Buddha, including his mother's vision of an elephant and a lotus blossom, his renunciation of worldly affairs, and his enlightenment. The Buddha statues show various postures, including teaching and meditation. Columns are richly carved with Buddhist scenes, elephants and lotus motifs, and there are also memorial columns with secular themes dedicated to rulers, artisans and religious leaders. The museum also exhibits Neolithic tools, metal axes and knives, beads, coins, caskets, ritual utensils and ornaments found at the site. More recent exhibits from the site include 13th-century Jain sculptures and 17th- to 18th-century statues of Ganesh, Nandi, Shiva and Shakti. The museum also has a model of the original site.

Open: Sat–Thur 9.30am–3.45pm.
Charges for admission and the launch.

Stupas

The earliest structure on the island was probably the Maha-chaitya uncased *stupa*, renovated in the 3rd century AD by the Ikshvashu princess Chamtisiri and believed to house relics of the Buddha. Nearby, a towering Buddha statue stands over the remains of a monastery foundation, which also has a small *stupa*.

Standing Buddha at Nagarjunakonda Museum

VIJAYAWADA

Two of the three great rivers of Southern India, the Krishna and the Godavari, flow through Andhra Pradesh to create a delta region called both 'the rice bowl of southern India' and 'the granary of Andhra'. The towns in the delta region have become the most important area of Andhra culture, producing some of the most famous Telugu authors.

Amravati

Once an important centre for Buddhism, Amravati saw the art of the Krishna delta reach its zenith in the 2nd century AD. This was the site for ancient Chintapalli, where a *stupa* was erected on the relics of the Buddha during the reign of the Mauryan emperor Ashoka. Ashoka converted to Buddhism in the 3rd century BC after seeing the death and destruction of Kalinga in his own quest for conquest, and Chintapalli was enlarged during the reign of the Savahanas from the 1st century AD onwards. The *stupa* has gone, but its base gives an idea of its size and circumference, and some scenes from the life of Buddha can still be seen. The ground plans of the monastic quarters remain at the site.

Most of the relics have been moved to the **Government Museum of Chennai** (*see pp102–3*) as well as to the Indian Museum of Kolkata and the British Museum in London; however, a handful remains at the site's archaeological museum. Here exhibits show various stages of development of the site from the 3rd century BC to the 12th century AD, and they include panels, railings and a number of sculptures. The sculptures comprise one of Buddha in his teaching posture with lotus symbols on his feet, curled hair and long earlobes; Tara, a Bodhisattva; and depictions of the *bodhi* tree – some of which are really fine – as well as chakras and lotus symbols. The collection also has relic caskets, pottery, coins and bangles from Amravati, and finds from other excavations in the Krishna district. A model of the *stupa* shows how it must have looked 2,000 years ago.

Rajahmundry

Rajahmundry, on the Godavari River, is known for its poets. Nannayya, often called the first poet or *adi-kavi* of Telugu literary history, is credited with starting the translation of the *Mahabharata* into Telugu, building the vernacular vocabulary to accommodate the words required for the Andhra *Mahabharata* about a millennium ago. It is also the home of author Kandukuri Veeresalingam, who brought about a revolution in the social structure of Andhra in the 1800s and 1900s. He campaigned for the rights of widows to remarry, and he opposed child marriage and the dowry system. He is credited with writing the first Telugu drama, and he also wrote the Telugu novel, *Rajasekhara Charitra*, as well as prose specifically for women.

Damerla Rama Rao Art Gallery at the Parade Grounds displays works by the late Andhra Pradeshi artist Damerla Rama Rao who died in 1925, and the gallery also hosts temporary art exhibitions. The **Government Archaeological Museum** on Godawari Bund Rd (*open: Sat–Thur 10.30am–5pm. Free admission*) has an interesting collection of sculpture, about 450 manuscripts (some of which are made of palm leaf), copper plates, Satavahan pottery, various coins, and archaeological finds from excavations in the Godavari district.

Rajahmundry has an airport and a railway station. There are places to stay and eat in the town.

Vijayawada

The headquarters of the Krishna district, Vijayawada is named after the **Kanakadurga temple** (*Indrikila Hill. www.kanakadurgatemple.net. Open: Fri–Wed 5am–9pm, Thur 9am–1pm & 4–9pm. Free admission*) whose presiding deity is also called Vijaya. The **Victoria Jubilee Museum** (*Bandar Rd. Open: Sat–Thur 10.30am–5pm. Free admission*) has finds from sites of the Krishna delta, while the nearby **Ondavalli Caves** exhibit 6th- and 7th-century columns and sculptures in niches.

240km (149 miles) southeast of Hyderabad, Vijayawada has an airport and a railway station. There are hotels and restaurants in the town.

Andhra Pradesh

Inside the Ondavalli Caves

Getting away from it all

The Southern States afford plenty of opportunities to escape from India's often overwhelming urban hustle and bustle. If you find solace in a soothing Ayurvedic massage, Kerala is the epicentre of the discipline, although treatment centres also abound elsewhere. Those seeking to commune with nature have a plethora of serene lakes, remote hill stations, and enviable birdwatching sites to explore, while the many wildlife reserves allow visitors to witness the animal kingdom at close quarters.

KERALA

It is easy to escape the crowded cities, towns and tourist centres of Kerala by taking an Ayurvedic programme, a houseboat cruise or a tour of wildlife reserves.

Ayurvedic resorts

A number of resort companies and hoteliers have developed health resorts to make the most of the popularity of Ayurvedic massages (*see pp34–5*).

Houseboats

Few visitors return from Kerala without taking a boat trip on the backwaters (*see pp40–41*). One means of travelling the backwaters is by chartered houseboat, which allows more flexibility to plan an itinerary than tour boats and ferries.

The price is based on the route, the facilities and services, the duration of the cruise, the size of the houseboat, the number of rooms, and the meals. Trips usually start at **Alappuzha**, **Kollam**, **Kottayam** or **Kumarakom**, but other

stretches, such as the backwaters near Thiruvananthapuram, Kozhikode and Bekal, are also good for cruising.
Government tourist offices and tour operators can be contacted to book a houseboat. Hotels and resorts of Kollam, Alappuzha and Kottayam district usually have their own houseboats or can arrange one according to your requirements.

Sanctuaries and National Parks of Kerala

Aralam Wildlife Sanctuary

This sanctuary, near Kannur, is home to elephant, mouse deer and sambar, besides a range of birds, but has not been developed for visitors.
This sanctuary has limited facilities for tourists. Contact the Aralam Wildlife Division, Irrity, Kannur District.
Tel: 0490 249 3160 for more information.

Chinnar

The Chinnar sanctuary comprises mainly deciduous forests and scrub flora. Permission to stay at the forest rest

houses is hard to obtain, and most visitors make the trip from Munnar or stay in simple highway hotels near Marayoor.
See p67 for more information.

Eravikulam National Park
The highlight of the 97sq km (37sq mile) Eravikulam National Park is the Nilgiri tahr, best seen in the Rajmalai range.
See pp66–7 for more information.

Idukki Sanctuary
This sanctuary is home to elephant, gaur bison and dhole wild dog. You can stay at Kottayam, 20km (12½ miles) away.

Kumarakom Bird Sanctuary
Set along the **Vembanad Lake**, this bird sanctuary is home to darters, cormorants, herons and egrets, and attracts migratory birds in winter.
Tel: 0481 252 5864. Open: daily 6am–5.30pm. Admission charge. Half-hourly buses leave from the KSRTC bus stand in Kottayam for Kumarakom.
Resorts at Kumarakom arrange boating and houseboats to tour the sanctuary.

Neyyar Sanctuary
The 128sq km (49sq mile) Neyyar sanctuary has a reservoir offering boat safaris. The sanctuary has elephants, tigers, bear and Nilgiri langur, but it can be difficult to obtain permission for trekking. Basic meals and accommodation are available locally.
Tel: 0471 232 2217. wildlife@sify.com.

Regular buses to Neyyar from the KSRTC bus stand in Thiruvananthapuram.
Kerala Tourism Development Corporation runs a hotel and cafeteria near the dam. Boats can be hired for a tour of the lake.

Parambikulam
This 285sq km (110sq mile) sanctuary is one of the finest places to view gaur (Indian bison) in Southern India. Accommodation can be a problem, so most visitors make a trip from Coimbatore or Pallakad, both more than 100km (63 miles) away.
Open: daily 7am–6pm (last entry 4pm). www.parambikulam.org; wildlifewarden@parambikulam.org. Admission charge. Bus: daily or twice daily from Pollachi, Parambikulam and Topship.

Peechi-Vazhani Sanctuary
This sanctuary's 125sq km (48sq miles) of forest is a good place to watch 60 species of birds including waterfowl. The mammals include elephant, tiger, panther and deer. The floral diversity includes 50 species of orchids.
Buses run to Peechi Dam from Thrissur. Permits from the Wildlife Warden at Thrissur. Tel: 0487 269 9017.

Peppara Wildlife Sanctuary
This 53sq km (20sq mile) sanctuary, near **Thiruvananthapuram**, has a fine reputation as a spot for birdwatching.
About 50km (31 miles) from Thiruvananthapuram. Contact the District Forest Office. Tel: 0471 232 5385.

Periyar National Park

Periyar is one of the leading tiger reserves of India. The mixed forest is set around a reservoir, for wildlife viewing by boat. *See p60.*

Shenduruny Wildlife Sanctuary

The Shenduruny moist deciduous forests, 66km (41 miles) from Kollam, span an area of about 100sq km (39sq miles). On the banks of the Shenduruny River are Mesolithic painted caves.
Contact The Wildlife Warden, Shenduruny Wildlife Sanctuary, Thenmala Dam PO, Thiruvananthapuram. Tel: 0475 234 4600.

Silent Valley National Park

This prime rainforest of 90sq km (35sq miles) is well known for its endangered monkeys. Palakad, 85km (53 miles) away, has accommodation.
Tel: 0492 422 2056.
www.silentvalleynationalpark.com.
Open: Dec–Apr 8am–5pm (last entry 2pm). Admission charge.

Thatekkad Sanctuary

One of the best bird sanctuaries in Kerala.
Tel: 0485 258 8302.
Open: Oct–Apr 6.30am–7pm. Admission charge.

Wayanad Wildlife Sanctuary

An impressive sanctuary of forests, swamps and grasslands.
See p81.

KARNATAKA

With its beaches, spas and wildlife reserves, all easily accessible from the popular tourist destinations of Bangalore, Mysore, Madikeri and Hampi, Karnataka makes a great destination as an escape from the more frenzied sightseeing itinerary.

Ayurveda, spas and health centres

Bangalore is the hub of India's health tourism industry, with spa resorts in and around the city offering Ayurvedic and other Indian treatments. Some also offer Thai, Balinese, Chinese and European treatments. Ayurveda and natural treatments are growing in popularity, and resorts and hotels at other destinations, such as Mysore, Mangalore, Kodagu and Hampi, have developed their own massage and treatment centres for travellers.

For more serious yoga and naturopathy programmes, the **Institute of Naturopathy and Yogic Sciences**, at Jindalnagar outside Bangalore, is regarded as one of the best of its kind.

Some interesting websites:
www.angsana.com (Angsana Oasis Spa Resort, Bangalore)
www.goldenpalmsspa.com (spa resort near Bangalore)
www.soukya.com (centre offering Ayurveda, homeopathy, naturopathy, yoga, reflexology, acupressure, acupuncture and other treatments at Whitefield, Bangalore)

www.ayurvedagram.com (Ayurvedic resort at Whitefield, Bangalore)
www.theleela.com (luxury hotel with spa and Ayurvedic centre)
www.summer-sands.com (beach resort with massage facilities at Mangalore)
www.ayurindus.com (Ayurvedic centre at Mysore)

Beaches

The stretch of coast between the Western Ghats and the Arabian Sea is followed by the Konkan Railway line and National Highway 17, which both travel the entire length of the Karnataka coast. This area is also known as the Sapphire Coast of India, and the route offers access to some of Southern India's prettiest beaches.

Devbagh Island

This island, 3km (2 miles) offshore from **Karwar** at the confluence of the Kali River and the Arabian Sea, is a must for beach lovers. It has log hut accommodation.
Karwar is on the main Konkan Railway line.

Gokarna

Gokarna's famous **Om Beach** is named after its curving stretch of sand in the shape of the Hindu *Om*, while **Kudle, Half Moon** and **Paradise beaches** are also popular. Gokarna is also a popular place of pilgrimage for Hindus.
Gokarna has a railway station, hotels and restaurants.

Mangalore

Sandwiched between one of the wettest stretches of the Western Ghats and the coastline, Mangalore is known for its busy port, industry, terracotta tile factories and colleges. It is also an interesting place to view historic monuments, including 10th-century temples, a 15th century church, and a

Getting away from it all

The beach at Murdeshwar near Gokarna

chapel with frescoes, as well as museums housing archaeological finds. Mangalore has a handful of popular beaches, such as nearby **Ullal**.

Mangalore has an airport and a railway station. There are good hotels in town and a resort at Ullal beach.

Udupi

Udupi is one of the most important Vaishnavite centres on the southwest coast of India. It is the birthplace of Madhva, a saint who set up monasteries in the town in the 13th and 14th centuries. The centre of religious activity here is the Krishna Temple.

A short drive from Udupi is the fishing port of **Malpe**, which is associated with Vasco da Gama. The explorer is said to have landed at St Mary's Isle and set up a cross before his historic landing at Kappad in Kerala. *Udupi is on the main Konkan Railway line.*

Waterfalls

Jog Falls is Southern India's highest waterfall. Altogether, it consists of four falls, the longest dropping about 293m (961ft), although the dam on the Sharavati River has reduced the flow. The falls are set in the spectacular countryside of the Western Ghats, being particularly impressive shortly after the monsoon, and the jungle-carpeted hills are a great place to do some hiking.

Jog Falls is about 2^1/$_2$ hours' drive from Hanovar Railway Station.

Wildlife reserves

Karnataka has five national parks and over 20 wildlife sanctuaries, including some of the most spectacular in Southern India. The hills are an important habitat for elephant, tiger and other endangered wildlife, and the following sanctuaries have been developed for tourism.

Bandipur National Park

This large national park is part of the **Nilgiri Biosphere Reserve**, along with **Madhumalai** (also spelt Mudhumalai) in Tamil Nadu, **Wayanad** in Kerala and Nagarhole (*see p136*), comprising an important wildlife corridor, especially for herds of elephant.

Tel: 0821 248 0901. Open: daily 6.30–9am & 3.30–5.30pm. Admission charge.

Bandipur is about 90km (56 miles) from Mysore. There is a good choice of accommodation, ranging from basic forest rest houses to privately owned wildlife resorts.

Bannerghata National Park

A popular day excursion from Bangalore, part of this national park has been developed for recreation, with a zoo, drive-through safari-park enclosures with big cats and herbivores, and picnic facilities. The surrounding forests are inhabited by a variety of mammals and birds.

Tel: 0802 842 9366. Admission charge. Bannerghata is about 26km (16 miles) from Bangalore.

Bhadra Wildlife Sanctuary

This wildlife sanctuary, situated in the wet forests along the Bhadra River, has been declared a Tiger Reserve, but it is notoriously difficult to spot one of these wonderful, elusive animals. Otters and crocodiles are often seen at the Bhadra Reservoir, while drives through the sanctuary could well result in sightings of elephant, gaur (Indian bison), a variety of deer and monkeys, and many species of birds. Leopard sightings are also possible.

Tel: 0826 222 2059;
dcfbhadra@yahoo.com.
Bhadra is 153km (95 miles) from
Mangalore. There is accommodation
near the reservoir.

Biligiri Rangaswami Hills

The **Biligiri Rangaswami Temple Wildlife Sanctuary** mainly comprises deciduous forests with patches of scrub and grassland, becoming increasingly evergreen at higher altitudes. While driving through the sanctuary, visitors stand a good chance of seeing elephant, sambar, spotted deer, wild boar and gaur, and occasionally also leopard and sloth bear. The sanctuary is also an excellent place for birdwatching, and you can expect to see eagles, thrushes, flycatchers and numerous other species.

Tel: 0822 622 2059. Open: 6am–6pm.
The temple sanctuary is about 86km
(53 miles) from Mysore, with
accommodation at K-Gudi nearby.

Dandeli Wildlife Sanctuary

This 475sq km (183sq mile) sanctuary is one of Southern India's most popular rafting destinations, with white-water and scenic raft trips organised on the Kali River. The river flows through moist deciduous and semi-evergreen forests, and ibises, darters and storks are likely to be sighted while on the river. Other bird species, such as hornbills, sunbirds, parakeets, woodpeckers and barbets, can often be spotted while walking or driving in the forests. Elephant, gaur, bonnet macaque, langur monkey, giant squirrel and leopard (including black mutant) could well be sighted here, and there is also a resident population of tiger.

Open: daily 6am–6pm. www.dandeli.com.
Dandeli is 125km (78 miles) from Londa
on the Konkan Railway line. There are
resorts and campsites near the Kali River.

Daroji Bear Sanctuary

This small sanctuary makes a good day excursion from Hampi, having a substantial sloth bear population in its scrub-forested hills. Bears are often

Sambar deer can be seen in many of Karnataka's reserves

sighted from the watchtower, below which there is a waterhole, and there are also chances of seeing wild boar, monitor lizards, jackals, Indian foxes and a number of species of scrubland birds. The sanctuary has been declared an Important Bird Area by the Indian Bird Conservation Network because of the presence of the yellow-throated bulbul, which is a globally threatened species. *Open: daily 6am–6pm. sammadkottur@indiainfo.com. Admission charge. Daroji is about 20km (12 miles) from Hospet, which has places to stay and eat.*

Rajiv Gandhi National Park, Nagarhole

Like Bandipur, this national park is located at the meeting place of the forested hills of Kerala, Karnataka and Tamil Nadu. Elephant, sambar, spotted deer, wild boar, gaur and hare are often seen during drives through the park, and there are also chances of seeing sloth bear, leopard and even tiger. As far as birdlife is concerned, Malabar pied hornbill, green imperial pigeon, grey jungle fowl, red spurfowl, crested serpent eagle, parakeets and flycatchers are regularly seen in the area. Large herds of elephant can usually be spotted at the Kabini River, especially in summer, and crocodiles, freshwater turtles, darters, cormorants and herons are other possible sightings from the coracle boats that are available for hire. *Rajiv Gandhi National Park. Tel: 0821 248 0901. Open: daily 6–9am & 4–6.30pm. Admission charge. Nagarhole is about 94km (58 miles) from Mysore. There are wildlife resorts and lodges at various places in the park, including Karapur near the Kabini River.*

Ranganthittu Bird Sanctuary
See p91.

TAMIL NADU

Rising from the coast to the peaks of the Western Ghats more than 2,500m (8,200ft) above sea level, Tamil Nadu offers a number of scenic resorts which provide relief from the bustle of its large industrialised cities and its crowded temple towns.

Andaman and Nicobar

Just over 1,000km (621 miles) offshore from the Tamil coast, the islands of Andaman and Nicobar have some of India's finest beaches and coral reefs, and they are popular diving and snorkelling destinations. Most of the islands are thickly forested with tropical vegetation.

The arrival point by air and sea is **Port Blair**, a town with a cellular jail where freedom fighters from India were imprisoned. The jail now houses a museum containing various instruments of torture, and it has nightly sound and light shows on its history. Port Blair also has an aquarium, an anthropological museum, a forest museum and a maritime museum, all of which are good primers for visits to the other islands. There is a popular beach at **Corbyn's Cove** out of town, and the road from here continues to **Chiriya Tapu**, with its pleasant beach and forested trails. Operators offer trips in glass-bottomed boats, as well as diving and snorkelling encounters in the bays and islands, including protected marine reserves, with boat transfers out of Port Blair. Another popular excursion is to **Mount Harrier**, reached by ferry from Port Blair. Here a forested path leads past tall tropical trees hung with vines, and it is an excellent spot for birdwatching and butterfly-spotting, while the view from the summit is breathtaking.

The most popular island for just relaxing is **Havelock**, reached by ferry from Port Blair. Here **Radhanagar Beach** is regarded by many as India's finest. Reached by a road through forests, the beach has perfect white sand with calm waters rich in marine life. *Planes operate between Chennai and Port Blair, which has a good choice of hotels. From here, passenger ferries connect to Havelock Island, which has a few good places to stay.*

Hill resorts

The **Nilgiris** or Blue Hills of Tamil Nadu are home to some of Southern India's most famous hill resorts. Developed for tourism, **Ooty** and **Kodaikanal** both provide a pleasant break from the plains, while those looking for peace and quiet can head for the tea-plantation town of **Conoor** or the coffee-plantation town of **Yercaud**.

Kodaikanal

At an altitude of about 2,100m (6,890ft) above sea level, Kodaikanal offers superb views of the hills. The centrepiece of Kodaikanal is its star-shaped lake, which is extremely popular for strolls, cycling and boating. Next to the lake, **Bryant Park** has paths meandering among attractive assortments of flowers and trees. The **Croaker's Walk** offers breathtaking views of the Nilgiri Hills, and the granite cliffs called **Pillar Rocks** are another natural attraction.

Getting away from it all

The countryside around Ooty

Popular excursions from Kodaikanal include **Fairy Falls** and **Bear Shola Falls**, and there is also a natural history museum on the road to **Madurai** that is worth a brief stop.

At one time a hill retreat for American missionaries and the British officers working in Tamil Nadu, Kodaikanal has attractive colonial-period houses. It is now a very popular hill resort for the people of Tamil Nadu and Kerala, and it can get very crowded during holidays.

Kodaikanal is about 120km (75 miles) from Madurai's airport. The city has a good choice of places to stay and eat.

Udagamandalam (Ooty)

Ooty is one of the best-known hill resorts in Southern India. At an altitude of about 2,200m (7,218ft), it was the summer retreat for most British residents of Southern India. While the town is now built up and can get rather crowded with visitors during holiday periods, there are still some quiet corners where peaceful walks are possible.

The **Botanical Gardens** are one of the town's main attractions. Laid out in the 1840s by gardeners from London, they sprawl over 16ha (40 acres) with a wide variety of trees and flowering plants that are a blaze of colour. The large lake attracts visitors who enjoy the area's walks and boating opportunities. The colonial buildings include **St Stephen's Church**, and **Civil Court**, while the **Ooty Club** has been a centre

of sports and recreation since the 1840s; the rules of snooker are said to have been laid down here.

The main natural attractions are outside Ooty town. **Dodabetta** is the highest peak of Tamil Nadu and can be seen from the road to **Kotagiri** from Ooty town. At just over 2,600m (8,530ft) above sea level, the summit has a viewing tower that provides a breathtaking view.

Southeast of the peak is **Conoor**, a town surrounded by tea-planted slopes. Less congested than Ooty, it is a delightful place to take a stroll, and it retains a strong hint of the British Raj with its colonial bungalows and plantation houses. Botanists should head for **Sim's Park**, which has an excellent display of flowers, as well as an attractive lake that you can walk around. There are good views from **Dolphin's Nose** near **Catherine Falls**, as well as from **Lamb's Rock**, and it is possible to get permission to visit some of the tea estates around town.

Another tea planters' town is **Kotagiri**, nearly 2,000m (6,561ft) above sea level, with good views of the surrounding hills. It is particularly known for its handicrafts.

Botanical Gardens. Open: daily 8am–6.30pm. Admission charge.
St. Stephen's Church. Open: Mon–Sat 10am–1pm & 3–5pm. Services Sun 8am & 11am. Free admission.
Sim's Park. Open: daily 8am–6.30pm. Admission charge.

Ooty is easily accessible by road from Coimbatore airport. The city has a good choice of places to stay and eat.

Yercaud

The town of Yercaud, in the **Shevator Hills,** is surrounded by coffee estates and fruit orchards. It is a good place for walking and trekking, with some very fine strolls around the lake.
Yercaud is easily accessible by road from Salem railway station.

Wildlife reserves

Tamil Nadu has a particularly rich diversity of wildlife habitats, ranging from the **Marine National Park** in the Gulf of Mannar, and the bird-rich saltwater lagoons along the coast, to the forests of the Nilgiris that are home to a fantastic variety of animals, birds and plant life.

Indira Gandhi National Park (Anamalai Hills), Topslip

Some of Tamil Nadu's finest forests are in this wildlife reserve. Some 958sq km (370sq miles) in size, the park's vegetation ranges from dry deciduous to evergreen and even sola (or swamp) rainforest. It forms an almost uninterrupted forest area with **Parambikulam** to its west and the **Eravikulam National Park** and **Chinnar Wildlife Sanctuary** to its south, all three in Kerala. This large forest corridor has created a habitat for endangered wildlife such as the Nilgiri tahr and the lion-tailed macaque, one of Southern India's

rarest monkeys. Most visitors to **Topslip** stand a good chance of spotting elephant, gaur (Indian bison), a variety of deer, the Nilgiri langur and bonnet monkey, and there are also resident tiger and leopard populations that are, understandably, a little more difficult to find. The park is good for birdwatching, with resident species including the Sri Lankan frogmouth, white-bellied treepie, Malabar trogon, white-bellied blue flycatcher, and numerous others.
Tel: 04259 222 5356. Open: daily 6am–6pm. Admission charge.
Topslip is about 75km (47 miles) from Coimbatore airport.

Madhumalai National Park & Wildlife Sanctuary

Tamil Nadu's most popular wildlife reserve, Madhumalai forms part of an important wildlife corridor with **Bandipur** and **Nagarhole** in Karnataka, and with **Wayanad** in Kerala, forming what is called the **Nilgiri Biosphere Reserve**. Mainly deciduous forest in the rain shadow of the Western Ghats, the sanctuary was for some time disturbed by an elusive poacher called Veerappan, but has since recovered. Large herds of

Herons are common around Vedanthangal Bird Sanctuary

elephant can sometimes be seen, including some old individuals with really long tusks, while gaur are Madhumalai's pride as they are known to reach an exceptional size here. Spotted deer are easily seen in good-sized herds, and wild boar is abundant. The sanctuary also harbours tiger, leopard, wild dog, flying squirrel, Malabar flying squirrel and other wildlife, but sightings of these are not easy. Together, Madhumalai and Ooty form a very interesting area for birdwatchers, especially for those who want to see the flycatchers of the Nilgiris.

Madhumalai is accessible from Coimbatore, and it has a good choice of accommodation.

Pulicat Bird Sanctuary

This large saltwater lagoon is renowned for its abundant flocks of flamingos, ducks, storks, avocet, sandpipers and other birds.

About 90km (56 miles) north of Chennai.

Vedanthangal Bird Sanctuary

This small reservoir is one of Southern India's most spectacular birdwatching sites. A path through the wetland area offers views of large flocks of spoonbill, open-billed stork, grey heron, night heron, pelican, darter, cormorant and numerous other birds that nest in the acacia trees. In the winter months the tank makes a very good spot to observe migrating ducks.

Tel: 0442 432 1471. Open: pre-dawn–11am & 4pm–sunset. Admission charge.

Vedanthangal is 86km (53 miles) south of Chennai. It is also a popular excursion from Mahabalipuram or Kanchipuram.

ANDHRA PRADESH

With a wide diversity of landscapes, from the Eastern Ghats to its long coastline, Andhra presents a number of attractive getaways from the densely populated regions of Hyderabad, Vishakhapatnam and the river deltas.

Beaches

The most popular beaches are those near **Vishakhapatnam**. It is a good idea to ask locally before entering the sea, as many stretches of the Bay of Bengal are not safe for swimming.

Vishakhapatnam has an airport and a railway station. There is a good choice of hotels in the city, as well as places to stay at Rishikonda, a popular beach. The museums and old buildings in the city, and the Buddhist sites nearby, are also worth a visit.

Birdwatching

Andhra's wetlands and grasslands are excellent birding areas. Below are some of the best sites near tourist destinations.

Hyderabad's lakes

Hussain Sagar is a large lake with a colossal granite Buddha that is one of the world's largest freestanding Buddha statues. **Shamirpet**, about 28km (17 miles) away, is a good place to watch storks, spot-billed duck and

Cattle grazing at Shamirpet Lake

other water birds. Other lakes, among them **Osman Sagar**, are popular recreational spots around Hyderabad.

Kolleru Lake

This large lake, with its neighbouring marshes, attracts a diversity of waterfowl.

Kolleru can be visited as a day excursion from Vijayawada.

Pakhal Lake

This large lake, situated in a deciduous forested sanctuary, supports large flocks of waterfowl.

Pakhal Lake is about 60km (37 miles) east of Warangal.

Pulicat Lake

This large lagoon is one of the top winter habitats on the east coast of India for shore birds, and it is a good place to see species such as spot-billed pelican, greater flamingo and painted stork.

The lake is near the Chennai–Nellore Highway and can be visited as a day trip from either.

Rollapadu Wildlife Sanctuary

Many species of grassland birds can be seen here, as well as eagles and other raptors, including the great Indian bustard. The sanctuary is also an important habitat for blackbuck or Indian antelope.

Rollapadu is near Kurnool, which has places to stay and eat.

Hills

Araku

Araku offers access to a number of coffee estates and tribal villages in the Eastern Ghats, and it is also home to one of Andhra's best tribal museums. **The Borra Caves**, with their spectacular stalactites and stalagmites, can be visited en route to Vishakhapatnam.

Araku is a scenic drive or railway journey (on one of the world's highest broad-gauge railway lines) from Vishakhapatnam. There are places to stay at Araku and Tyda on the road to Vishakhapatnam.

Horsley Hills

Situated at about 1,200m (3,937ft) above sea level among the deciduous forests of the Eastern Ghats, this resort is a popular destination for walks, weekend trips and birdwatching opportunities.

About 140km (87 miles) from Tirupathi, a temple town with an airport and railway station, Horsley Hills has places to stay and eat.

Shopping

Shopping in India can be an exciting experience. The four states featured in this book have a rich tradition of handloom weaving, metalwork, wood- and stone-carving, and other handicrafts, as well as arts such as painting and contemporary sculpture. Southern India also grows high-quality spices, tea and coffee.

How to shop

At established shops, prices are generally fixed and there is no real room for bargaining, although some shops will give you a deal for large purchases. It may be a good idea to check the prices at different shops before buying, as the discounts may vary. Shops usually announce 'clearance sales', 'discount sales', 'off-season sales' and 'festival discounts' in the newspapers or declare them on banners.

At street-side markets and at flea markets the prices are usually marked up and there is considerable room for bargaining. In tourist centres, vendors generally hike the price up and you might do well by halving the asking price and then reaching an agreement. Walk away slowly in order to gauge the response of the vendor, and you will usually be called back for further negotiation. Shop owners and sales people can be very persuasive, so it is important to be firm and not be swayed.

What to buy

Southern India is known for its textiles, such as the silk sarees of Mysore in Karnataka, the silk sarees and brocades of Kanchipuram in Tamil Nadu, the ikat-woven cotton and silk sarees of Andhra Pradesh, and the silk and cotton fabrics from the northern districts of Kerala.

The tradition of metal sculpture continues at bronze-casting workshops in central Tamil Nadu. Bidriware, the art of engraving on a metal alloy before blackening and polishing, was developed in Bidar in Karnataka by Persian artisans from the Sultan's court. Attractive boxes, vases and other items are produced at Hyderabad in Andhra Pradesh.

Mahabalipuram is India's stone-carving capital, and high-quality sculptures, mainly Hindu idols, are produced in its workshops. Wooden items range from the painted toys of Kondappali and Ettikoppakka of Andhra and Chennapatnam near Bangalore, to the fine ebony, rosewood and sandalwood sculptures of Karnataka.

Jewellery is another popular buy, especially in the markets of Hyderabad, where pearl necklaces and locally made glass bangles are sold, and in Tamil Nadu, known for its silver ornaments. For jewellery made from precious metals and gemstones, it is best to buy from larger shops that will certify that they are genuine.

Andhra Pradesh is also known for folk narrative paintings on both cloth (Kalamkari) and on furniture (Nirmal). Tribal artefacts made from bamboo and terracotta can be bought at Araku in Andhra, and the embroidery of the Lambani Banjara community can be purchased in Hampi, in the northern districts of Karnataka, and in parts of Andhra. For contemporary art, the galleries in the major cities have exhibitions, and auctions from time to time.

Southern India is also a good place to buy spices such as cardamom, cinnamon, ginger, pepper and nutmeg, and tea and coffee. These are available at shops, markets and estate outlets. Vendors in Kerala also sell attractive packs of spices that make good souvenirs or gifts.

Pondicherry is known for its fine handmade paper, and for a range of other crafts.

It is illegal to take genuine antiques out of India without proper licensing, but you can find good copies in the markets.

Where to buy

Government-owned emporia are generally safe bets for genuine quality at fixed prices, but sometimes private shops also claim to be government emporia. Hotel shopping malls and big shops also guarantee quality, although they may be more expensive. Some non-governmental organisations (NGOs), registered charities, communes and artisans' cooperatives have retail outlets promoting the work of artisans or disadvantaged people.

Some factories are also open for visitors to see their processes, such as weaving, coir-making or tea production, and it is then possible to buy from the factory outlet.

There is no dearth of markets in India. They are good places to look for fresh fruits, vegetables, meats and fish, and to find bargains.

Old city bazaars are atmospheric and full of colour, and the maze of streets and alleys is lined with vendors, open-air stalls and shops selling a wide range of products for the locals, including utensils, jewellery, clothes and food.

KERALA
Kochi
Art
Chitram Art Gallery
MG Road, Ernakulam. Tel: 0484 235 7012.
Dravidia Art & Performance Gallery
Kalvatty near Fort Kochi.
Galleria Mareecheka
Chittoor Road.

Galleria Synagogue
Mattancherry. Tel: 0484 222 2544.

Books
Idiom Books
183 Synagogue Lane, Jew Town.
Tel: 0484 222 5604.
DC Books
Kurian Towers, Banerji Road,
Ernakulam. Tel: 0484 239 1295.
Paico *MG Road, Ernakulam*
Business Centre. Tel: 0484 236 1020.
www.paicoindia.com

Handicrafts
Kairali
MG Road. Tel: 0484 235 4507.

Jewellery
Alapatt Fashion Jewellery
MG Road, Ernakulam.
Tel: 0484 235 2149.
Temple Fashion Jewellery
2330 Muthodt Royal Square.
Tel: 0484 238 0422.

Textiles
Parthas Textiles
PB 1774 MG Road.
Tel: 0484 237 4175.

Thiruvananthapuram
Books
DC Books
Statue Junction. Tel: 0471 245 0133.
Higginbothams
MG Road. Tel: 0471 233 1622.
India Book House
MG Road. Tel: 0471 247 5443.

Modern Book Centre
Near GPO, MG Road.
Tel: 0471 247 8826.
Prabhat Book House
Vanchiyoor. Tel: 0471 247 1533.

Handicrafts
Bee Orchid
TC 14/1343 Indeevaram,
Paris Road.
Gift Corner
MG Road.
Handloom House
Near East Fort. Tel: 0471 247 2886.
Hastakala
Indian arts and crafts.
Off MG Road. Tel: 0471 233 8463.
Kairalai
Opposite Secretariat. Tel: 0471 247 5627.
Natesan's Antiqarts
Opp. Ayurveda College, MG Road.
Tel: 0471 233 1594.
Partha's
Powerhouse Road. Tel: 0471 246 1949.
SMSM Institute
YMCA Road. Tel: 0471 233 0298.

KARNATAKA
Bangalore
Books
Gangarams
72 MG Road. Tel: 0802 558 1618.
Higginbothams
68 MG Road. Tel: 0802 558 6574.
LB Publishers
90–91 MG Road. Tel: 0802 558 7621.
Motilal Banarasidas
236 III Block, 9th Main Road, Sri Ranga,
Jayanagar. Tel: 0802 654 2591.

Prism Books
11th Main Road, IV Block, Jayanagar.
Tel: 0802 663 7527.

Handicrafts
Cauvery
49 MG Road. Tel: 0802 559 7511.
Central Cottage Industries Emporium
144 MG Road. Tel: 0802 558 4515.
www.cottageemporiumindia.com

Textiles
Deepam Silk
67 MG Road. Tel: 0802 558 8760.
Karnataka Silk Industries
Corporation
Jubilee Showroom, 44/45 Leo Complex,
Residency Road Cross.
Tel: 0802 558 2118.
Mysore Saree Udyog
294, 1st floor, K Kamraj Road.
Tel: 0802 509 8821.
www.mysoresareeudyog.com

TAMIL NADU
Chennai
Books
Higginbothams
814 Anna Salai. Tel: 0442 851 3519.

Handicrafts
Gujurat Emporium
67 Royapettah High Road.
Tel: 0442 498 4440.
Spencer Plaza
Anna Salai. Tel: 0442 849 1122.
SIPA'S Craftlink
Kodambakkam High Road,
Nungambakkam. www.sipa.in

ANDHRA PRADESH
Hyderabad
Books
AA Hussain & Co
Abid Road. Tel: 0402 320 3724.
Bookionics
Gandhi Gyan Mandir Lane, Kothi,
beside VHP Building.
Tel: 0402 344 5603.
Higginbothams
Near Lal Bahadur Stadium. Tel: 0402
323 7918.
Walden
Greelands Road, Begumpet.
Tel: 0402 340 3344.

Handicrafts
Lepakshi
Opposite telephone exchange,
Musheerabad. Tel: 0402 321 2902.
www.lepakshihandicrafts.gov.in

Textiles
Pochampally Silks and Sarees
Tilak Road. Tel: 0402 475 5216.

Local handicrafts sit alongside Ayurvedic
powders used in Hindu rituals

Arts and crafts of Kerala

Patronised by the princely states and temple builders, the artists and artisans of Kerala excelled in painting and sculpture.

Painting

The painting traditions that began in rock-cut temple caves more than 1,000 years ago reached their zenith in the temples of the 16th to the 18th centuries, such as Ettumanoor, the palace of the Rajas of Kochi, and even in the churches of Kerala. Drawing heavily from the style of the Pallava, Hoysala and Vijayanagar School, these murals were distinctive in their use of colour, line and subject matter.

Some people believe that the origins of Keralan mural painting can be traced back to *Kalamezhuttu*, ritual drawings of deities and *mandalas* (geometric patterns), made with coloured powder. Each colour derives from natural sources such as rice flour, turmeric, leaves and burnt husk, and is applied using the thumb and forefinger.

Sculpture

Like painting, woodcarving developed in Kerala with patronage from the landed families and the temple builders. Sandalwood, teakwood and rosewood sculpture, especially those of Hindu deities, can be seen in a number of cities and towns. Toys, lacquered woodwork, Kathakali models and wooden furnishings are sold at emporia and in the markets.

Metalwork

The traditional medium for metal sculpture is a blend of gold, silver, copper, iron and tin (called *panchaloha*), but bronze sculptures of deities also became popular because of their durability. Bell metal, comprising mainly copper, is commonly used today for metal crafts, such as temple bells, which are said to have a special chime when struck. One of the most famous centres for metalwork is

Carved sandalwood figures

Shiva images are available all over Southern India

Nadavaramba, near Irinjalakuda, which manufactures oil lamps and cooking utensils.

Gold jewellery

For the people of Kerala, gold symbolises light, eternity, wealth and purity. Gold jewellery is therefore present at auspicious occasions, particularly births and weddings. In the past, the design of the jewellery often denoted the community to which the wearer belonged, but now patterns are universal and range from the plain to the elaborate. The Nagapadam is a serpent pendant, once popular with Nair women, and generally in the shape of a cobra hood. The Kasumala is a gold coin necklace, usually depicting the Goddess Laxmi, although some kasumalas also portray British royalty.

The Tali necklace tied around the neck of a bride has an Om if she is a Hindu and a cross if she is Christian. The Cheruthali necklace is an ornament of the Namboodiri Brahmin women, and the Oddiyanam waist belt is extremely popular among Tamil Brahmins. The Vanki is a forearm ornament generally used during weddings, while gold earrings, especially the bell-like jhimka, are also popular in Kerala. The Mekka Mothiram was a popular ornament of the Christian community in Kerala, and the Mangamala is a necklace with a mango motif. The jasmine-shaped pendant is called a Mullamottu, and the Palaka is a gold ornament set with green glass. The jewellers of Kerala rarely set other stones into gold jewellery, and although contemporary designs are coming into fashion, most of them are still based on traditional patterns. No visitor to Kerala, especially to the central region from Kochi to Kozhikode, can fail to notice the number of hoardings advertising gold jewellery.

Other handicrafts

Kerala is well known for weaving of various kinds, including coir weaving, reed weaving, screw-pine mat weaving, and grass mat weaving, as well as embroidery and lace making. Some weaving units have started using jute as a substitute to coir and cane.

Entertainment

Entertainment in Southern India generally revolves around traditional performances of dance drama, Carnatic music and Kerala's martial arts, Kallaripayettu. In the modern cities of Bangalore, Hyderabad and Chennai, rock and jazz bands, Latin American dances and other international performance arts are becoming popular at luxury hotels, nightclubs, lounge bars and pubs.

ART GALLERIES

The art galleries in the museum complex at Thiruvananthapuram hold regular exhibitions of contemporary artists. Kochi has exhibitions and performances at the **Galleria Synagogue**, the **Dravidia Art & Performance Gallery**, the **Art Café** and **Kashi**.

CINEMA

India has one of the world's largest film industries. While Hindi films transcend regional borders, doing well in most states of India, regional language films in Andhra Pradesh, Tamil Nadu, Karnataka and Kerala are also extremely popular. Film stars have achieved almost cult status in the south; some have even been elevated to the levels of gods. The films' popularity has made the actors politically influential and some have won positions in government assemblies. They are often called upon for canvassing during state and national elections.

An Indian film is usually a larger-than-life escapist fantasy, though in recent times stories have become more realistic. While tragedies were popular in the early years of the Hindi film industry, the 1970s and 1980s saw the advent of 'masala movies', which followed set formulae that appealed across cultural boundaries. Common themes were: a hero, the 'angry-young man', fighting evil against all odds with a love interest thrown in; a reunion between brothers separated during childhood; or one of the 'love triangle' themes involving two friends in love with the same girl, with one making the 'supreme sacrifice' for his friend.

Spanning three hours including an interval, a typical Hindi film features a little of everything – romance, comedy, action, melodrama, religious piety and song sequences at the drop of a hat, usually filmed in spectacular settings such as snowy peaks, desert dunes or beaches. Many films are shot in foreign locations.

Today, the film industry is going through something of a revolution with film makers targeting the Hindi-speaking audience in the UK and USA, and in other countries where tickets are more expensive than in India and DVDs are in greater demand. The increased revenues have resulted in better production standards and more subtle storylines.

As Hindi films continue to be popular, there is usually a cinema hall in or near every city or town. The standards of cinema halls are improving in the larger cities like Chennai, Hyderabad and Bangalore, with many new multiplexes offering more legroom and more comfortable seats.

Thiruvananthapuram is the site for an International Film Festival, and the city has many cinemas showing Indian films, as well as some English-language films.

∧ traditional ensemble

CULTURAL CENTRES FOR MUSIC, DANCE AND FOLK ARTS

Kochi

Art Kerala
Kannanthodathu Lane, Valajambalam, Ernakulam. Tel: 0484 236 6231.

Cochin Cultural Centre
Souhardham, Manikath Road, Kochi. Tel: 0484 236 7866.

Kerala Kathakali Centre
Cochin Aquatic Club, River Road, Fort Kochi. Tel: 0484 221 5827.

See India Foundation
Kalathiparambil Lane, Ernakulam.

Bangalore

Nrityagram Dance Village
Hessaraghatta. Tel: 0802 846 6313.

Chennai

Kalakshetra Arts Village
Dr Muthulakshmi Road.

Music Academy
TTK Road, Dr Radhakrishnan Salai. Tel: 0442 811 5619.

Hyderabad

Shilparamam
Madhapar.

Kalaripayattu

It is possible to see students learning the martial art of Kalaripayattu or masters practising at gymnasiums called kalaris in almost every city or town in Kerala. Demonstrations are often available if advance notice is given – the price is based on the number of people attending. You can also make appointments for Ayurvedic treatments, and short-term courses are run at some kalaris.

ENS Kalari Centre, *Nettoor, Kochi.*
CVN Kalari, *P.O. Edakkad, Calicut. Tel: 0495 239 1808;
email: sudhakarant@yahoo.com*
CVN Kalari Sangham, *East Fort, Near Sri Padmanabhaswamy Temple, Thiruvananthapuram. Tel: 0471 247 4182.*

Kathakali

One of the four main classical styles of India, the dance drama follows certain norms but is dynamic and has accepted various changes over the years, such as replacing the mask with stiff make-up. In order to make the dance drama form more popular, shorter versions have been created for tourists.

The ritualised dance drama form of Kathakali is performed at the temple theatres of Kerala, but these are rarely open for non-Hindus. A good alternative, however, is to see a performance at a cultural centre.

Hotels at Thiruvananthapuram, Kovalam and Kochi also stage Kathakali shows on a regular basis: ask at the tourist offices for information.

Music

Kerala is known for its Carnatic music, and you should be able to find out about performances in all the major cities. Ghazals and other Hindustani music is popular in Kozhikode.

A Kathakali dancer in full regalia

Children

India is a family-oriented society where children are welcomed, and this warmth is extended to those travelling with them. Children are very popular in India and most Indians will bend over backwards to help you. Children are welcomed in most hotels and restaurants, religious places and at the various tourist sites and monuments. However, travelling with children in India does involve a few hazards of which you need to be aware.

Accommodation

It makes sense to find a good hotel for your base while in India. Most chefs will prepare food to your requirements and there is usually a mini-bar with bottled water and snacks. Hotels will happily supply an extra bed or a family room at a supplement, although children below the age of ten are not usually charged for occupying a room. Some hotels and resorts are geared up for children, with play areas, toddlers' pools, indoor games, movies, competitions and special menus, but it is best to find out about the facilities when you book. Some hotels may be able to arrange babysitters.

Food

It may be a good idea to carry baby food with you, particularly if your child has particular favourites which may not be available. At hotels, resorts and restaurants there is generally a large menu, with good options for children. Eggs, biscuits, bread, butter, cheese, chocolate, bottled drinks, ice cream, packaged and canned foods are generally available everywhere.

Health

Those travelling with babies and children need to be careful. Besides all the necessary vaccinations (*see pp183–4*), children should also be protected against diphtheria, whooping cough, mumps, measles and Hepatitis B.

Local people love children and will offer them sweets and fruits, so it is important to be vigilant about this when travelling with children. It may help to explain to them that the child has to be on a special diet when travelling in India.

On the road

Long journeys with children in India can be difficult, so it's best to base yourself in just one or two places. If you are renting a car, buying a child's car seat is a good idea. Bathrooms are rarely clean; taking a portable toilet seat with you may help. There are grocery stores on the roadside, and snacks are available on board the trains, but it's best to pack some snacks for your journey. Biscuits, chocolates and soft drinks are easily available.

Your children may be disturbed by the attention lavished on them by Indians, so you need to be prepared for this.

Packing

Nappies and toiletries are available in Indian cities, but emergency supplies are recommended. Also, make sure you bring any medicines which you may need, as well as a first-aid kit. It is a good idea to pack some toys and books to keep children amused.

Things to do

India does not have any of the large amusement parks that children look forward to visiting. However, children will probably enjoy the general liveliness of India, where getting around in auto-rickshaws, trains, ferries and chartered boats can be fun. Rides on elephants, camels, ponies and boats are also great favourites.

Backwaters

Cruising the backwaters can be great fun for children, and speedboats can also be hired for short journeys.

Beaches

Children will enjoy the beaches of Kerala and Karnataka. Kovalam is a popular beach destination, while beaches at Veli and Varkala near

Madras Crocodile Bank Trust, Chennai

Thiruvananthapuram, Marari near Alappuzha, and those near Kochi, Thallesseri, Kannur and Bekal in Kerala, and near Mangalore and Gokarna in Karnataka are also popular for day trips. Before entering the water, check that it is safe to swim or paddle there; some beaches have lifeguards who will show you the safest areas.

The beaches along the Bay of Bengal coast of Tamil Nadu and Andhra Pradesh are generally less safe for swimming than those on the west coast of India, but they are very pretty (*see pp130–41*).

Hill resorts

Children are likely to enjoy hill stations such as Ooty and Kodaikanal that have lakes with boating facilities, pony riding trails, bicycle hire, parks and gardens. Hotels at these hill resorts are usually geared up for children, as they are very popular with Indian families.

In town

All cities and towns have parks and gardens, with paths for a pleasant stroll and with areas for children to play.

Shopping

The Indian bazaars and handicraft emporia can be fun for children. Locally made dolls dressed in the attires of different states of India, Kerala's papier mâché Kathakali masks, handcrafted wooden toys and miniature boats are favourites. However, make sure that the toys you buy are safe for children.

Wildlife reserves

Seeing big animals is exciting for children. The launch tours at Periyar Lake can be thrilling, especially in the morning or evening when elephant herds, gaur, sambar, bears, monkeys, fishing eagles and turtles are most likely to be seen. Drives in Wayanad in Kerala, Nagarhole, Bandipur and the Biligiri Rangaswamy Hills in Karnataka, and Mudhumalai in Tamil Nadu also offer good opportunities to see elephants, a variety of deer and monkeys, and possibly even a leopard or tiger. Coracle rides with the locals on the Kabini River in Karnataka are also enjoyable, as they can get closer to elephants and crocodiles. There are good accommodation options at the reserves. Check the safety regulations at each park, as it may not be safe to venture into certain areas.

Zoological parks

Hyderabad has one of the best zoos in Southern India, with large enclosures, drive-through safari parks to see big cats from mini-buses, a nocturnal house, a reptile park and a café. Mysore's zoological park also has well-designed enclosures that re-create the natural habitat of each animal or bird. Other important zoos are at Chennai, Thiruvananthapuram and Vishakhapatnam. Chennai also has a well-known snake park at Guindy, a wooded park in the city where deer and other animals can be seen, and a crocodile park.

A monkey in Chinnar Wildlife Sanctuary

Sport and leisure

Although sports are not generally associated with India, except, of course, for Himalayan mountaineering and cricket, they are nevertheless a popular form of entertainment. All kinds are on offer, from spectator sports to those especially developed for tourism, such as watersports and adventure activities.

Large hotels and resorts have sports facilities including swimming pools, and many smaller ones have indoor games facilities such as pool tables. The clubs are the best places for sports and leisure, but entry is usually restricted to members. Some clubs have reciprocal arrangements with those elsewhere, while some offer temporary membership, and hotels may be able to arrange admission to a club nearby. Some clubs also have residential rooms, which can be an alternative to staying at hotels, but you may need to be introduced by a member. You could also ask about government-run sports facilities that are open to the general public.

Sports facilities
Adventure and watersports
Dandeli National Park in Karnataka is a popular destination for rafting, canoeing and kayaking on the River Kali. The rafting activities on offer range from scenic floats through the forests, which are good for birdwatching and occasional wildlife sightings, to strenuous white-water rafting at the falls. There are resorts and camps near the entrance to the national park run by Indian Adventure and **Jungle Lodges and Resorts Ltd** (*www.junglelodges.com*).

Angling
Some hotels and resorts have their own ponds, private lakes or backwater inlets where they allow fishing on catch-and-release or you-catch-we-cook basis. Most of them have fishing rods, but it may be a good idea to bring your own equipment. The prized fish of the Kerala backwaters is *karimean*.

The High Ranges Angling Association at Munnar is helpful in giving information and obtaining licences for fishing in Kerala's lakes and rivers. Most globetrotting anglers visit Southern India to fish for the mahseer, a group of carp that ranks among the largest and toughest freshwater fish in the world. Permits to catch the mahseer are usually given on a catch-and-release basis, as this is an endangered group of fish. Jungle Lodges and Resorts Ltd operates camps at mahseer fishing sites on the Kaveri River. The resorts and camps in Kodagu district can also help enthusiasts to get permits from the region's wildlife association for mahseer fishing.

Basketball

Basketball is a popular game, mainly at school and college level.

Billiards and snooker

Billiards and snooker are popular in India. Most clubs have a billiards room and some hotels have pool tables.

Cricket

Cricket is the most popular sport in India. Crowds gather in hotels and public places to watch international fixtures on TV, especially if the Indian team is playing. You can observe cricket practice at stadiums and in campuses, as well as informal games played on open ground, and children playing with a bat and ball even in narrow streets. You may even be invited by locals to join a friendly game. At competitive level, cricket is a serious business, and Indian clubs invite foreign teams to play or tour other countries. All the four states in this book have cricket associations. Some of India's leading test and one-day international players are from Bangalore and Hyderabad.

Volleyball at the roadside in Thrissur

You can play cricket on any surface

Cycling

Southern India offers a variety of terrain for bicycle touring. Indian bicycles are good for short distances and local sightseeing, but they are not very comfortable for serious touring on hilly roads or rocky paths. You can either join a group tour with everything taken care of by the operator, or bring your own bicycle, preferably a mountain bike. If you bring a bicycle, carry more spares than you think will be needed, including oil and a pump.

Indian bicycles can be hired at most cities, towns and villages at very nominal prices. Imported bicycles are available only at very popular tourist destinations.

Football

Football is a popular sport in Kerala. Its football clubs excel in national tournaments, and they usually also have members in the national team.

With the advent of international TV channels in India, soccer is widely followed in the country, and most locals will discuss the last World Cup if they know you have any interest in the game.

Golf

Kerala has some seven- to nine-hole golf courses and plans are afoot to develop an 18-hole one, but admission is usually reserved for club members and their guests. The Trivandrum Golf Club's clubhouse was established about a century ago by the Maharaja of Travancore. Munnar has golf courses for the plantation staff and management, and local hotels may be able to help you find a local member who can introduce you as a guest. Bangalore and Kodagu district in Karnataka, and Ooty in Tamil Nadu, have golf courses but similar restrictions may apply. Bangalore has a number of 18-hole golf courses, including the historic Bangalore Golf Club founded in 1876, the Karnataka Golf Association's course and the Eagleton Resort. Hyderabad, Chennai and Mysore also have 18-hole golf courses. You can find out about any local tournaments that allow foreigners to participate.

The Trivandrum Golf Club, Kowdiar, Thiruvananthapuram. Tel: 0471 243 5834.
High Range Club, Munnar.
Tel: 0486 523 0253.
Cochin Golf Club, Bolgatty Island.
Tel: 0484 275 0908.

Scuba diving and snorkelling

Visitors to Southern India in search of good diving sites and unspoilt marine areas for snorkelling may find them in Lakshadweep, a cluster of islands offshore from Kerala, or at Andaman off the eastern coast of India. For those visiting Lakshadweep, there are flights from Kochi that land at Agatti, from where the resort on Bangaram Island generally arranges helicopter or ferry transfers for their guests.

Port Blair on South Andaman Island receives flights from Chennai. Most Port Blair hotels can arrange snorkelling trips and there are tours from the harbour to some of the good reefs nearby. Dive operators usually have offices or booking agents at Port Blair or at Havelock Island.

Check a company's certification and safety standards before joining a tour or course.

Bangaram Island Resort, Lakshadweep (Casino Group, Kochi. Tel: 0222 404 2211).
The Society for Promotion of Recreational Tourism and Sports in Lakshadweep, Willingdon Island, Kochi. Tel: 0489 626 2255.

Book diving or snorkelling trips through your hotel or a registered operator

Swimming pools

Almost all resorts and most of the big hotels have a swimming pool. By regulation, swimming pools at Indian hotels and resorts are shallow and prohibit diving. They have separate changing rooms, with showers, for men and women. Towels are provided and many hotels have smaller pools for children, as well as Jacuzzis® next to the main pool. Pools are cleaned regularly, and it is a good idea to follow the specified swimming pool opening times to avoid chemicals and soaps. Some hotel pools permit non-residents, for an admission charge.

Swimming pools at clubs and sports complexes usually follow international competitive standards regarding size and depth, and many have diving boards.

Tennis, badminton and squash

Most of the bigger resorts and hotels, and almost all clubs, have facilities for these popular games. Tennis and badminton are very popular in Bangalore, Hyderabad and Chennai.

Volleyball

Volleyball is very popular in Tamil Nadu and Kerala, and is also played at school and college level in the other states of India. Some beaches also have volleyball courts for visitors.

Parasailing on the Keralan coast

A tranquil pool at a Munnar resort

Health clubs and spas
Ayurveda, yoga and meditation
With the increasing international interest in these ancient Asian disciplines for physical and spiritual wellbeing, several hotels and resorts have made yoga, meditation and Ayurvedic therapies available to their guests. Both short- and long-term courses are offered, and at some upmarket resorts there are daily sessions for beginners at fixed hours.

For more serious yoga students, the beginner and advanced courses at ashrams and government-approved institutions may be preferable. Neyyar near Thiruvananthapuram, and Nileshwar near Kasaragode, are among the most renowned places for yoga instruction.

See Neyyar under Thiruvananthapuram on p30.

Health clubs
Many hotels and resorts have health clubs with a gym, sauna and steam bath. Use of the gym is usually free for hotel residents. Most health clubs are managed by a team of supervisors responsible for maintaining the equipment and assisting guests. A few hotels and resorts also have daily aerobics sessions and weight-training instructors. The health clubs generally have separate sections for men and women, but some may also have different timings.

Long-staying visitors can also become members of health clubs with qualified instructors. Inspect the equipment and hygiene standards before joining a programme.

Sport and leisure

Walking

Southern India offers plenty of variety for those who love walking. There are narrow roads through the old quarters of most cities and towns, village paths that offer a glimpse of rural Indian life, coastal roads through palm groves, winding roads and paths in the hills, mountains and in plantation areas, and more strenuous treks in the Western Ghats.

The Keralan coast

Birdwatching

Birdwatching in Southern India is particularly rewarding. The long coastline of Andhra Pradesh and Tamil Nadu is very good for spotting flamingoes, pelicans and shore birds. The Coringa Wildlife Sanctuary comprises mangrove forests at the estuary of the Godavari, and you can also spend time at the large lagoon of Pulicat, the lagoons and salt pans of Point Calimere (Kodikkarai), 94km (58 miles) from Thanjavur, and the lagoons of Rameshwaram Island.

The Western Ghats offer excellent birding opportunities, especially at: the hill stations of Ooty and Kodaikanal, where many species characteristic of the Nilgiri hills can be seen; Munnar and its nearby wildlife reserves; the Nilgiri Biosphere Reserve stretching from Mudhumalai through Bandipur and Nagarhole to Wayanad; Periyar Lake and its surrounding wildlife reserve; and the Salim Ali Bird Sanctuary off the Kochi–Munnar highway.

Ranganatithu Bird Sanctuary and Kokarebellur near Mysore, and the Vedanthankgal and Karikili wetlands near Chennai, are good places to get close-up views of breeding birds. Rollapadu is perhaps the best sanctuary in Southern India to see the Great Indian Bustard, and is also home to the endangered Lesser Florican. The sanctuary is one of the largest roosting sites for harriers in Southern India.

A Long-tailed Shrike surveys the scene

Food and drink

Visitors will find a delightful variety of food in Southern India. While seafood such as crab, lobster, crayfish, prawns, shrimps, squid, clams and mussels are abundant on the Arabian Sea and Bay of Bengal coasts, you will also find lamb, mutton (goat), beef, pork, chicken and duck, and a variety of fresh vegetables, cooked in the locally grown spices.

Where to eat

Indian food can be a lot more spicy on its home ground than at curry restaurants abroad; Indians use chillies liberally. Hotels, resorts and restaurants in the tourist centres are accustomed to travellers and invariably prepare food to suit the foreign palate. The cooks are pretty accommodating about preparing food according to any specific dietary or special requests.

Outside the big hotels and restaurants, it is generally safe to eat where the food is freshly prepared and well cooked, including the street-side *dhabas*.

Health issues

One of India's greatest health hazards for visitors is its drinking water. Drinking straight from a tap, or using tap water for cleaning teeth, is an open invitation to water-borne diseases, as the public water supply is often contaminated. Bottled water is widely available, but check the seal properly and crush the bottle before disposing of it so that it can't be refilled. At restaurants, ask for the sealed bottle to be opened in front of you. If you are visiting someone's home, ask if the water is 'purified'. Carry water sterilisation tablets and a filter just in case you visit somewhere where bottled water is not available.

Fruits, vegetables, cold meats and fish that have been exposed to flies or washed in dirty water are risky even in big hotels. Shellfish is not recommended unless you know that it is very fresh.

Drinks

Tea, or *chai*, is made in Indian homes and restaurants by brewing tea leaves, milk, water and sugar. This is usually a safe drink to have, and it is often easily available at street-side kiosks, railway stations and on trains. *Masala chai* includes powdered spices such as ginger, cardamom or cinnamon. For tea in a pot, with milk and sugar served separately, ask for 'service tea' or 'English tea'.

Coffee is also served white, brewed with milk and sugar unless specified. Espresso and cappuccino are becoming popular at cafés and coffee shops, and South India is famous for its local-style filter coffee.

Another popular beverage in India is *lassi* or *chaas*, which is buttermilk made by churning yoghurt. As this contains water, you need to give the waiter purified water from which to make it. Similarly, make sure that fruit juices are served without water or ice.

Breakfast
At hotels, breakfast is usually a lavish buffet, but it can also be a set American, Continental or Indian menu. Even at smaller hotels, packaged cereals with milk, fried eggs or omelettes and buttered toast form the usual breakfast spread, with a further choice of North Indian or South Indian breakfast items.

If you are eating out at street-side restaurants, the usual breakfast options are *puri* (deep-fried whole wheat rounds) with vegetables, *parathas* (Indian whole wheat bread cooked and usually stuffed with potatoes and other vegetables), *idlis* (rice dumplings), *wadas* (deep-fried savoury doughnuts) or *dosas* (savoury rice pancakes, usually stuffed with potatoes, and served with a lentil soup, *sambar*, and a coconut chutney).

Indian food
Tandoori is very popular in the Southern States, this refers to marinated mutton, chicken or fish barbecued in an earthenware oven and usually served as kebabs or *tikkas*. The main courses of a North Indian meal (also called Mughlai or Punjabi and usually listed separately on restaurant menus) are rich, with liberal use of cream and nuts. The South Indian restaurants and cafés are usually owned by the Brahmin community and serve pure vegetarian food, which means they do not serve eggs or alcohol, although concessions are made in places likely to attract tourists. *Udupi*, generally associated with authentic Brahmin cuisine of the Karnataka coast, is commonly seen as a prefix or suffix to the name of eateries across the Southern Indian states. These are good places to get not only popular snacks but also a set meal of vegetables, *rasam* (peppery soup), *sambar* (lentil soup, usually with a coconut base), dumplings, pickles, chutneys, apalams or papadums, rice and sweets like *payasa* (rice pudding) or *holige* (fritters). Most *Udupi* food is made without onions or garlic.

Darshinis are Southern India's regional fast-food cafés serving inexpensive South Indian snacks and meals. They are very popular in Bangalore. Mangalorean restaurants are strong on seafood cooked with a coconut base. Kodagu district is known for its pandi curry (pork) and rice dumplings. 'Tiffin Rooms' at Bangalore, Mysore and other cities are known for their excellent *masala dosa* (potato-stuffed crisp pancakes) for breakfast and set meals.

Andhra's *bhawans* or restaurants offer a variety of food from across Andhra Pradesh, ranging from Hyderabadi food, which is strongly influenced by the Middle-Eastern and Mughal origins of the Nizams of Hyderabad, to the food of the fertile Krishna and Godawari deltas, that of the drier areas of the Deccan, and the coastal cuisine around Visakhapatnam. Typical meals or *thalis* at these *bhawans* are hot and spicy with lots of chillies and pungent pickles as accompaniments, though you could ask for milder versions in the tourist areas. The meals usually contain a lot of leafy vegetables. A sour-tasting leaf called *gongura* or *ambada* is an important ingredient of most soups (*rasam, dal* or *sambar*) and is also ground with red or green chillies into a fiery chutney. You will also find mutton or chicken dishes blended with a gravy or dry curry base of green leafy vegetables like spinach (*palak*), gongura or fenugreek (*methi*). Dry-fried fish or pepper-coated chicken is commonly served as a starter. Curried prawns are popular in coastal Andhra. Hyderabad is well known for its *biryani*, steam-baked saffron-flavoured rice layered over meat, *haleem* (ground meat), paya soup and paratha breads.

In Tamil Nadu, many eateries serve set vegetarian meals which are generally simple and mildly spiced. The meal usually comprises a variety of vegetables, sambar, rice, rasam, papadums, sweets and sometimes chappatis. Chettinad restaurants, also gaining popularity across Tamil Nadu, serve a variety of meat dishes in spicy gravies that are strong on pepper, chilli, garlic and ginger.

Meal or *thali*

A 'meal' or a *thali* refers to a simple set menu with a fixed price served to everyone. It is usually good, quick, reasonably priced and freshly prepared. A vegetarian meal usually includes vegetables, chappatis, pulses, rice, pickles, yoghurts and sauces, and occasionally a local sweet. A *thali* is served on a metal platter, with the individual items in separate little bowls. Non-vegetarian meals usually include mutton, chicken or fish dishes.

Ice cream

Well-known brands are Vadilal and Amul, plus international names such as Walls and Baskin-Robbins. Amul also offers Indian ice cream called *kulfis*. Avoid ice cream from hawkers.

Fruits

Papaya, pineapples, guava, jackfruit, oranges, mangoes, grapes and sweet limes are among the many fruits grown in Southern India, and other fruits such as apples and pears are also available. You can buy fruit and vegetables such as cucumbers from markets, street-side vendors and hawkers with pushcarts anywhere in India. Bargaining helps bring down the price. Peel the fruit before eating it, or at least wash it in purified water.

WHERE TO EAT

Prices

The following categories are based on the price of an average meal per person, excluding drinks:

★   Rs 150 to Rs 300
★★   Rs 300 to Rs 500
★★★ Rs 500 and above

Bangalore

Amrawati ★
Andhra meals.
MG Road.

Mavalli Tiffin Rooms ★
South Indian food.
Lalbagh Road.

Aromas of China ★★
Chinese restaurant.
Richmond Circle.

Koshy's ★★
Popular café with western and Keralan dishes.
St Mark's Road.

Spiga ★★
Mediterranean.
Vittal Malay Road.

Chennai

Ceylon Restaurant ★
Sri Lankan cuisine.
12 Kennet Lane.

Saravana Bhavan ★
Southern Indian chain.
293 Peter's Road.

Annalakshmi ★★
Vegetarian food.
Anna Salai.

Copper Chimney ★★
North Indian food.
Cathedral Road.

The Rain Tree ★★
Chettinad meals.
Taj Connemara, Binny Road.

601 ★★★
Top international fare.
Park Hotel, 601 Anna Salai. Tel: 0444 627 6000.

Peshawari ★★★
Northwestern cuisine.
Welcomgroup Park Sheraton, Cathedral Road.

Hyderabad

Angeethi ★
Indian food.
Road No 1, Banjara Hills.

Backwaters ★
Keralan food.
Road No 57, Jubilee Hills.

Bawarchi ★
Hyderabadi cuisine.
RTC crossroads.

Fusion 9 ★
International meals.
Road No 1, Banjara Hills.

Southern Spice ★
Andhra food.
Road No 3, Banjara Hills.

Deccan Pavilion ★★
Regional dishes.
ITC Kakatiya Sheraton, Begumpet.

Touch of Class ★★
Andhra food.
Lakdikapul.

Kochi

Kashi ★
Popular restaurant with an 'art café' gallery.
Burgher Street.

Malabar House Residency ★
Italian and Indian food.
Near St Francis Church, Fort Kochi.

Chariot Fort ★★
A popular café.
Near Children's Park, Princess Street.

History Restaurant ★★
Historically themed menu.
Brunton Boatyard, Fort Kochi.

Old Courtyard ★★
International menu.
Princess Street.

Thiruvananthapuram

Cafe Magnet ★
A popular café.
Women's and Children's Hospital, Thycaud.

Kalavara Family Restaurant ★
Popular eatery with good fish.
Press Road.

Orion ★★
Multi-cuisine restaurant.
Hotel Residency Tower, Press Road.

Land of spice: coastal cuisine

Keralan cooking uses coconut milk, coconut flesh or coconut oil in most dishes. There are regional variations and differences between the preparations of the Moplah community of Malabari Muslims, the Syrian Christians and the other Malayalis. Arabian influences are obvious in the Moplah cuisine, where dried fruits and nuts are used for gravies and *biryani*. English influences are apparent in the dishes of Syrian Christians.

Breakfast may include *puttu*, a steamed rice cake that is sometimes served with bananas or fish. *Idiappams* are steamed rice noodles topped with ground coconut and often served with curried vegetables or meats. *Appam* is a flat, chappati-like rice cake with crispy edges, and is a popular breakfast item.

A chef at the Park Hotel, Chennai

Typical vegetarian dishes, common to all communities, are *avail*, mixed vegetables in a grated coconut sauce with or without fruits and nuts, *thoren*, vegetables fried or steamed with coconut, mustard and occasionally also green papaya, and *olen*, a coconut-based bean and gourd curry. These are served as accompaniments to rice, with *sambar*, a lentil soup with vegetables, and *rasam*, a flavoured broth. *Pachkkary shtew* is a typical tangy vegetable stew, very popular in central Kerala, especially among the Syrian Christians. It is usually eaten with *appam*.

Other vegetarian favourites are cheera curry, which is spinach curried with coconut milk, and *vendekka varathathu*, which is roasted okhra. Vegetarian Keralan meals, influenced by Ayurvedic principles, are popular at Ayurvedic resorts.

As is to be expected from a state with 44 rivers, backwaters, innumerable lakes and a long coastline, fish and seafood is a mainstay of the cuisine of Kerala. Sardines, kingfish, squid, tiger prawns and crabs are the usual catches along the coast, while karimean or pearl-spot is the classic catch of the backwaters. The lakes also yield sizeable fish catches. Fish is usually prepared in coconut curry (*meen pahichadhu*), in chilli-hot curry (*meen vevichatu*), with sour fruit and chillies (*meen kodampuli*), in thick curries (*meen mappas*), in grated coconut and spices curry (*meen peera*), in a mango curry (*mathi curry*), in a banana leaf (*meen pollichathu*) or pickled. Other popular fish dishes are *meen moily* in a mildly spiced coconut curry or *meen varathathu*, fried fish. Curried prawns are also very popular.

Chicken curry is very popular and there are many versions such as *kozhy thenga varutharachathu* (curried with fried ground coconut) or *kozhy varathathu* (fried chicken) at restaurants in Kerala. Ducks are often reared by the people living along the backwaters. You can get *thengapal chertha tharavu*, which is curried duck in coconut milk, or *varutha tharavukari*, which is duck roasted with dry red chillies, accompanied with tapioca or *appam*.

Mutton (goat) is eaten more often than lamb in India. *Attirachi mappas* is a typical mutton curry of Kerala. Mutton *biryani*, steam-baked rice layered on mutton and boiled eggs, is extremely popular in northern Kerala.

Among the four states of Southern India, you are most likely to find beef on restaurant menus in Kerala because of the sizeable Muslim and Christian populations. *Mattirachi*

Street-food stall, Thiruvananthapuram

peralan is beef in a hot and spicy curry. Some Malayali Hindus also eat buffalo beef.

Pork is eaten by the Hindus and Christians of Kerala.

The various types of bread include *Kerala parathas*, fried wheat flour, pancakes such as *appam*, which is made from rice with a spongy centre, or the crisp *pathiri*. *Puttu* is a popular breakfast made from rice-flour dough. Rice noodles are called *idi-appam*.

Towards the end of the meal, the people of Kerala eat yoghurt-based dishes such as coconut-flavoured curd called *pachadi*. *Payasam* is a popular pudding made from sugared rice or vermicelli.

Hotels and accommodation

Southern India has a huge variety of accommodation, ranging from family-run guesthouses to upmarket resorts. Visitors can expect to find a hotel that suits their needs and their budget in most towns. However, hotels in India suffer from a number of problems that visitors may not have experienced elsewhere, such as dust, mosquitoes and other insects, power cuts and water shortages.

Price categories

Hotels are graded from one-star to five-star deluxe, with categories of four-star and above given by the central government authorities and the lower star classifications by the state government. Hotels are judged on a number of pre-determined standards, from ambience and room size to the qualifications of the staff, services and facilities.

Five-star deluxe hotels have extensive facilities, including modern rooms, round-the-clock room service, swimming pool, bar, 24-hour coffee shop, and restaurant. Five-star and four-star hotels are a cut below the five-star deluxe hotels, while three-star hotels maintain reasonably good standards without the frills of a five-star deluxe.

Budget stays

India has many modestly priced hotels. Most of them are located near railway stations, bus stations or near the market, and standards vary considerably. Some can be great value for money, while others are downright dirty.

Before booking into a really low-priced hotel, it is important to inspect the rooms to check the standards of cleanliness and to see that everything works.

Forest lodges

The forest department has lodges and resthouses inside most Indian wildlife reserves. Like the other government guesthouses, these too are beautifully located but are rarely well managed and can be difficult to book prior to arrival.

Privately owned lodges, resorts and camps are generally located near the entrance to or in peripheral areas of the reserves. These are organised for visitors to the wildlife reserves.

Government guesthouses

Government guesthouses, such as the Circuit Houses in cities, and the Public Works Department Resthouses, which are located outside the cities and towns, are often grand colonial buildings with equally impressive rooms. Most of them have highly desirable locations, but unfortunately many of them are poorly managed and maintained. Moreover, rooms are generally reserved for government officials, so finding accommodation can be difficult.

Heritage hotels

Buildings built before 1935 that have been opened for visitors are called heritage hotels in India. This is not a homogeneous concept, and it covers a variety of types of accommodation, from five-star deluxe palace hotels to bungalows run by the owners.

In Kerala, heritage hotels, such as Ayisha Manzil at Thalasseri and Harivihar at Kozhikode, are still partially occupied by their owners. Other old residences, including River Retreat at Cheruthuruthy and Malaabar House Residency, have been converted into hotels. A unique concept in Kerala is the relocation of old wooden houses to new sites, such as beaches and backwaters, to create 'heritage resorts'. Surya Samudra, Somatheeram and Nikki's Nest at Chowara south of Kovalam, and Coconut Lagoon at Kumarakom, are almost entirely comprised of transplanted old wooden buildings. Palaces in Mysore have been converted into hotels offering luxury facilities.

Plantation houses

It is possible to stay at working plantations, in Munnar, Kodagu district, Kumily near Thekkadi (at the entrance to the Periyar Tiger Reserve), and on the way from Thekkadi to Munnar. These plantations all have

Lalitha Mahal Palace Hotel, Mysore

Luxury pool at an upmarket resort

converted heritage houses, as well as newly built resorts.

Railway retiring rooms

Most railway stations have private rooms and dormitories that are handy for travellers. These are in high demand and are almost always full.

Tourist bungalows

The government-supported tourism corporations of Kerala, Karnataka, Tamil Nadu and Andhra own and manage tourist bungalows in their respective states. These can be good-value options for travellers, but standards vary considerably. At some destinations, they could be the only places to stay.

Andhra Pradesh Tourism Development Corporation *www.tourisminap.com*
Karnataka State Tourism Development Corporation *www.kstdc.nic.in*
Kerala Tourism Development Corporation *www.ktdc.com*
Tamil Nadu Tourism Development Corporation *www.tamilnadutourism.org*
Pondicherry Tourism *www.tourism.pon.nic.in*

Upmarket resorts

Resorts at the beaches or hill stations have a special attraction because of their location. They provide idyllic settings for those who want to indulge in the vast range of facilities available. Some of the popular resorts are at the beaches of Kovalam and

Marari, the backwaters around Kumarakom, the hill town of Munnar in Kerala, the hill stations of Ooty and Kodaikanal, and the beaches near Mahabalipuram in Tamil Nadu. Such resorts are heavily booked in the winter months from October to March, so early advance reservations are recommended.

Central bookings

Casino Group of Hotels

This regional group has some of the best upmarket resorts in Kerala and Lakshadweep.
Willingdon Island, Kochi.
Tel: 0484 266 8221.
Email: casino@vsnl.com

Edassery Group

This group has a hotel, Eastend, in Munnar, as well as some marvellous colonial bungalows in the surrounding hill country.
Temple Road, Munnar. Tel: 0486 523 0451.
www.edasserygroup.com

ITC Hotels Limited

Hotels at Bangalore, Chennai, Hyderabad, Vishakhapatnam and Port Blair.
10 Institutional Area, Gurgaon–122001.
www.welcomgroup.com

Jungle Lodges and Resorts Ltd

Lodges and camps in Karnataka.
2nd Floor, Shrungar Shopping Centre, MG Road, Bangalore–560 001.
www.junglelodges.com

Marriott

The upmarket Marriott chain has hotels across India under its various brands, including Courtyard, Lakeside Chalet and Renaissance.
www.marriott.com.

Olive Brook

Intimate hill station resort with excellent food and cooking classes.
Pothamedu, Munnar. Tel: 0486 523 0588.
www.olivebrookmunnar.com

The Park Hotels

Hotels in Bangalore, Chennai and Vishakhapatnam.
Sales & Marketing Office, Apeejay Business Centre, 3 Dinshaw Vachha Road, Mumbai 400 020.
www.theparkhotels.com

Tranquil

As well as a relaxing coffee plantation retreat, this firm also operates a hotel in Bangalore.
Sultan's Bathery. Tel: 0493 622 0244.
www.tranquilresort.com

Treehouse accommodation in the hills of Kerala

On business

India is an important exporter of gems and jewellery, textiles and ready-made garments, marine products, agricultural products, electronics and engineering goods. The country entered the new millennium as a leading centre for information technology, with significant software exports and allied services.

Bureaucracy

Despite the reforms introduced by Congress ministers in the 1992 budget, and the present government's promises of a good business environment, bureaucracy still exists in India and you need to be patient with the lengthy procedures involved in government business.

Business dress

Most Indians dress formally for meetings, but the dress code is rarely very rigid. Men should usually wear a smart shirt and trousers, and women should dress equally smartly.

Business etiquette

Business meetings in India usually start with an exchange of introductions and business cards. Social and personal interaction is the norm in India, and most visitors are extended warm hospitality with invitations for lunches and dinners with business associates and their families. The system is, however, formal and hierarchical. Men are addressed as Mr, and women as Mrs or Miss. Academic and military titles, such as doctor or captain, are respected. Indian employees address their seniors as 'sir' or 'madam', and they do not smoke in front of them.

Meetings tend to be lengthy, and Indians usually spend a lot of time over negotiations and discussions. It is a good idea to check things several times, to make certain that you are understood and that others agree with you (Indians rarely argue with foreign visitors, considering it impolite).

Business hours

Most government offices and nationalised banks work from 10am to 6pm on weekdays and shorter hours on Saturdays (some offices are closed on the second and fourth Saturdays of the month). Private establishments have longer hours.

Business services

Most five-star hotels are equipped with business centres, secretarial services, conference halls and messaging services. Telecommunications, internet access and photocopying facilities have improved considerably in India in the last few years, although they do not always compare well with those of more developed countries.

Postal services are inconsistent, but there are courier services at Thiruvananthapuram, Kochi and Kozhikode.

Food and drink

Hindus rarely eat beef, while Muslims and Jews do not eat pork. Even non-vegetarian Muslims may decline meat at a restaurant if it is not *halal* (prepared according to Islamic law). Most Muslims and some Hindus do not drink alcoholic beverages.

Language

Most executives, business people and high-level government officers speak good English.

The bustling port of Kochi is the scene of much trade and business

Practical guide

Arriving

International

Anna International Airport in Chennai is the main gateway to Southern India. Bangalore and Hyderabad are also served by international flights. The airports of Kerala mainly receive international flights from Middle-Eastern countries.

Domestic

Domestic airlines, such as Indian Airlines, Jet Airways and Sahara, connect the gateway cities of Mumbai and Chennai with Southern Indian destinations.

Air Deccan *www.airdeccan.net*
Air India *www.airindia.com*
GoAir *www.goair.in*
Indian *www.indian-airlines.nic.in*

Jet Airways *www.jetairways.com*
Kingfisher Airlines
www.flykingfisher.com
Paramount Airways
www.paramountairways.com
Sahara Airlines *www.airsahara.net*
Spicejet *www.spicejet.com*

Airports and customs

At the time of writing, visitors are allowed to bring into the country personal items, alcoholic drinks up to a maximum of 1 litre, 50 cigars, or 200 cigarettes or 250g of tobacco, and duty-free gifts up to a maximum value of Rs 4,000.

Any expensive personal effects or equipment such as binoculars and cameras should be registered for re-export. Keep registration numbers

Overloaded bus, Karnataka

The hills of the Western Ghats

handy, especially for laptops, cameras and other expensive equipment, as these are required when you fill in the re-export form. There is a departure tax for international flights, but some airlines add it to their fare.

Airline offices

Air France *Jet Air Pvt Ltd, 43/44 Thapar House, Montieth Road, Egmore, Chennai–600008.*
Tel: 0444 2855 4916, 0444 2855 4894. Fax: 0444 2855 3428.
Air India *19 Rukmani Lakshmibathy Road, Egmore, Chennai–600008.*
Tel: 0444 2855 4477, 0444 2855 4488.
American Airlines *Jet Air Pvt Ltd, 43/44 Thapar House, Montieth Road, Egmore Chennai–600008.*
Tel: 0444 2859 2564, 0444 2859 2649, 0444 8592 915. Fax: 0444 2854 0703.
British Airways *Sigma Wing, 177 Anna Salai, Chennai–600002. Tel: 0444 2860 4680, 0444 2256 0952. Fax: 0444 2855 1601, 0444 2860 3803.*
Cathay Pacific Airways Ltd *Spencer's Travel Services Ltd, Desabandhu Plaza, 47 Whites Road, Royapettah, Chennai–600014. Tel: 0444 4214 0941.*
Continental Airlines *STIC TRAVELS (P) LTD, Temple Tower, 476 Anna Salai Nandanam, Chennai–600035.*
Tel: 0444 2433 0211.
Delta Airlines *Aviation Travels Pvt Ltd, Desa Bandu Plaza 47, Whites Road, Chennai–600014. Tel: 0444 2852 5655, 0444 2852 5755. Fax: 0444 2852 3430.*
Japan Airlines *Hotel Ambassador, Pallava, 53 Montieth Road, Egmore, Chennai–600008.*
Tel: 0444 2859 2333, 0444 2859 2333. Fax: 0444 2859 2334.
Lufthansa *167 Anna Salai, Chennai–600002. Tel: 0444 2256 9393.*

Malaysian Airlines *Meenambakkam, Chennai 600002. Tel: 0444 2256 0084.*
Qantas Airways *TRANS WORLD AIRLINES, G3, Eldorado Building, 112 NH Road, Chennai–600034.*
Tel: 0444 2827 8680, 0444 2827 8649.
Fax: 0444 2824 0608.

Climate

Southern India has a tropical climate, with temperatures ranging from 18°C to 35°C.

Seasons

April to June (summer) is the hottest period and November to February (winter) is the coolest. The coast can become humid in the warm months. The interior hills of Munnar and Periyar Tiger Reserve are more pleasant than the coast in summer, but they can be chilly in winter.

The monsoon

The southwest monsoon blows in from the Arabian Sea and is condensed by the cooler climes of the Western Ghats, causing torrential rains, lashing waves and powerful winds in early June. There is another wet spell in November and December, which is caused by the retreating monsoon from the eastern Bay of Bengal.

Clothing

Loose-fitting light cottons are most suited to the warm and humid weather of Kerala, but it is a good idea to carry a jacket or a sweater for the evenings,

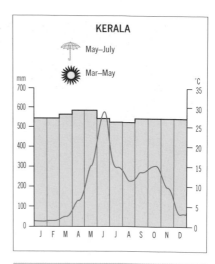

**WEATHER CONVERSION
CHART**

25.4mm = 1 inch
°F = 1.8 × °C + 32

especially if destinations in the Western Ghats, such as Wayanad, Munnar and Periyar, are part of your itinerary. Long-sleeved clothes in light colours provide some protection from mosquitoes.

Wear comfortable shoes and sandals that allow your feet to breathe. Laundry is inexpensive and rarely takes more than 24 hours, but delicate clothes should be washed personally.

Electricity

Electric current is 230–240 AC, 50 cycles. Electric power cuts are frequent but usually short-lived. Bring a surge protector to protect any electrical equipment from power fluctuations. Most hotel rooms have both two-pin and three-pin sockets.

The climate in Kerala is ideal for growing tea

Practical guide

Getting around

Boats

Boats provide a good way of seeing the landscape along the backwaters. You can take a tourist cruise or charter a whole boat.

Buses

Buses are an economical and convenient way to reach places off the railway network in Kerala, but they are rarely the most comfortable means of transport. The Kerala State Road Transport Corporation (KSTC) has buses connecting the cities, towns and most of the important villages, but you may have to change if visiting remote places or travelling very long distances. Signs at bus stands and on the buses themselves are sometimes in Malayalam, but you are likely to find English-speaking passengers willing to help and interpret. Bus stations at the cities and at most of the bigger bus stands have information counters. Most buses have a section of seats reserved for women.

Private buses are usually more comfortable. Some operators run air-conditioned coaches, express buses and overnight 'sleeper' coaches (with bunks), but you must be prepared for loud music. In recent years, better quality air-conditioned European coaches have begun to operate between

Southern India gets hit annually by the monsoon

Bus station at Idukki

cities. Bookings are computerised in many cities, and it is possible to reserve seats in advance.

Local buses run in cities such as Thiruvananthapuram, Kochi and Kozhikode, as well as the large towns. They are a cheap means of transport, though by no means the quickest or most comfortable option.

Cars and motorbikes

Hiring a car with a driver provides opportunities to travel off the beaten track and see the beautiful scenery of Kerala. Most drivers speak English and the local language, and can act as interpreters to ask directions or interact with locals. The rates are calculated on the basis of hours or days, with a proportionate kilometre allowance. If you hire a car for more than a day, the 'night halt charge' includes the driver's expenses. The driver will also expect a tip at the end of the tour.

Motorbikes are usually available to hire at tourist destinations. An alternative is the scooter, which has a lockable place for small items and a spare tyre on the back. Mopeds generally have no gears and are suitable only for travelling short distances.

You should always check the terms and conditions before hiring (third party insurance is compulsory in India). An international driving licence is advisable.

Bring a helmet with you or buy one in Kerala. Most travellers hiring motorbikes usually bring their own gloves, leathers, boots and other protective clothing.

Cycling

Bicycles are really only good for local travel in cities and towns, unless you are a real enthusiast who wants to make long-distance journeys along the coast or attempt challenging rides in the hills. Bicycles can be hired in most cities, towns and villages; they are heavy and do not have gears, but they are good for seeing some of the quieter areas of town, or for travelling on narrow streets. Some operators now offer imported mountain bikes for hire in popular tourist centres.

On the roadsides you will find repair shops that are reasonably priced. Before you set off, check the tyres and the general condition of the bicycle, and that the bell and lights work. It may be a good idea to bring lights with you, plus a cord to strap down your luggage, as these are not easily available in India. Those travelling with children may find it useful to bring a basket along or get one made. Do not leave your rucksack or any other luggage on the bicycle, as it could be an invitation to

A boat on the backwaters brimming with happy daytrippers

thieves. If you bring your own bicycle with you, carry plenty of spares and a repair kit.

Ferries

Public ferries can be a convenient and economical means of seeing the backwaters. Ferries from Ernakulam, Fort Kochi and Willingdon Island in Kochi carry small vehicles such as motorbikes.

Taxis and rickshaws

Taxis are available at airports, railway stations and at taxi stands in the cities. Make sure you negotiate the rate for the trip before setting off.

Auto-rickshaws are noisy and uncomfortable three-wheel vehicles, with a driver in front and a bench or seats for two or three passengers at the back. They are more economical than taxis and convenient for negotiating the crowded and narrow streets because of their smaller size.

Trains

Trains are a reliable and usually punctual method of travel in Southern India. Overnight train travel saves both hotel expenses and time, and Indrail passes are convenient if you are planning to spend a lot of time on the rail network in India (although expensive for local travel within Kerala).

Train travel is popular and advance reservation is essential. The ticketing is computerised and there is a tourist window for those paying foreign currency at some stations, which can save the trouble of standing in queues.

A few trains, such as the Rajdhani Express, have air-conditioned first-class carriages with coupés or four-bedded cabins. Two-tier and three-tier air-conditioned sleeper cars have curtains along the aisles, and the folding bunks have reading lights and bedding provided. Second class is overcrowded and uncomfortable, with narrow, hard benches. Some trains have air-conditioned cars with seats. There are tables that fold down from the chair back in front, magazine racks and overhead luggage racks.

Vendors sell bottled water, soft drinks and snacks on board and at stations, and simple meals are served on most trains, but it's a good idea to carry an adequate supply of food and water.

For up-to-date details of train services, consult the bi-monthly publication the *Thomas Cook Overseas Timetable*, available to buy online at *www.thomascookpublishing.com* or by telephoning *01733 416477*.

Health

Most visitors are immunised against polio, typhoid, tetanus, TB, meningococcal meningitis and Hepatitis A and B before a visit to India.

Take dietary precautions to prevent diarrhoea and intestinal upsets, and make sure that you slap on the sun block, as many travellers suffer sunburn and heatstroke from spending time on the beaches without adequate protection. If you get bitten by a dog, monkey or other animal, an anti-rabies shot is essential. Ticks and leeches are common in the Western Ghats, and tick bites can cause typhus.

Hospitals and medical facilities

Generally, Southern India has good doctors and there are clinics and hospitals in the cities and in most large towns.

A Shiva shrine

Malaria

Malaria is a serious problem, so see your doctor before leaving home. If you have any symptoms, consult a doctor. Also, protect yourself against mosquito bites by covering yourself completely at night and using repellents.

Pharmacies

There are medical stores in cities, large towns and most villages. You will also find medical stores on the highways. The stores usually have local equivalents of most medicines, but carry an emergency supply of essential and prescribed medicines.

Internet

India is a computer-oriented society and a number of email and internet access centres have appeared in Kerala.

Media

You will have access to Mumbai or Bangalore editions of national English-language dailies, such as the *Times of India* and *Indian Express,* as well as locally published English dailies. News magazines such as *India Today*, *The Week* and *Outlook* are also available at newsstands and bookstores.

Almost all hotels have satellite TV in their rooms, with a choice of channels for Indian and international programmes. Besides the foreign channels, you can also access Indian news in English.

The cooler hills around Munnar

Money

The Indian currency is the rupee, which is divided into units of 100 *paise*. Notes are printed in denominations of Rs 1,000, 500, 100, 50, 20, 10 and 5, while coins are minted in Rs 5, 2, 1, 0.50, 0.25, 0.20 and 0.10. Indians write Rs 100,000 as Rs 1,00,000 (one *lakh*), with 100 *lakhs* making a *crore*.

Currency exchange

It is not possible to order rupees in your home country, so you will need to change currency on arrival at the airport. Money exchange is not really a problem in India as banks, hotels and licensed private moneychangers or authorised dealers will happily change

dollars or sterling for rupees. Collect your encashment certificate, which will help you when you need to reconvert currency. The certificates also help you to pay in rupees at tourist quota counters at railway stations.

Traveller's cheques

Thomas Cook's traveller's cheques are widely accepted for exchange and as payment at hotels, and they are a relatively safe way of carrying money.

Credit cards

Almost all star-category hotels and resorts, expensive restaurants and established shops accept Visa and MasterCard.

Internet cafés, Kochi

Tipping

It is customary to tip 10 per cent at restaurants, Rs 10 to Rs 20 each to hotel porters, and Rs 50 to Rs 100 a day to drivers.

Passports and visas

A visa is essential for all visitors to India except those from Nepal and Bhutan. It is valid for six months from date of issue and can be obtained from the Indian embassy in most countries. You should also carry a set of photocopies in case you lose the originals.

Indian embassies abroad

Australia

3–5 Moonah Place, Yarralumla, Canberra.

Canada

10 Springfield Road, Ottawa, KIM IC9.

New Zealand

10th floor, Princess Tower,
180 Molesworth St, Wellington.

South Africa

4th Floor, The Old Station Building,
160 Pine St, Durban 4001.

UK

India House, Aldwych, London
WC2B 4NA.

USA

2107 Massachusetts Avenue, NW,
Washington DC 20008.

Photography

See p23.

Post and freight

Postal services in India range from excellent to very unreliable. Send letters, postcards and parcels only from the big cities and towns and make sure the covers are franked in your presence at the counter. Important mail should be sent by registered post with a registration receipt and an attached acknowledgement card to be returned signed. Airmail and speed-post services are available at most large post offices. Stamps can be bought at the counters. Poste restante facilities, which most travellers find reliable, are available at most post offices. Leading courier services like DHL have offices in important destinations like Kozhikode, Kochi and Thiruvananthapuram, which a local courier service, called *angadia*, operates to smaller towns and villages. It is possible to send air-freight from airports like Kozhikode, Kochi and Thiruvananthapuram. The railways and some bus services also take domestic cargo.

Safety and security

Southern India is a fairly safe place to travel, although Goa's reputation as a drugs market does attract undesirable elements to the region, and there have been some high-profile incidents involving tourists. Remain alert and avoid out-of-the-way places at night. The vast majority of Indians who approach you during your travels will do so out of nothing more than friendliness and curiosity; however, bear in mind that being in a foreign environment can make tourists vulnerable.

Theft

Petty thefts are not uncommon in India. A money belt is a good way to carry handy cash, and an interior pocket is good for small valuables, spare cash and photocopies of documents.

Unattended baggage is an invitation for theft; keep a padlock and chain with you to secure your baggage to any immovable object if you need to leave it for any reason.

On trains, there are wires below the bunks to which you can secure your baggage with a chain and padlock.

Sustainable tourism

Thomas Cook is a strong advocate of ethical and fairly traded tourism and believes that the travel experience should be as good for the places visited as it is for the people who visit them. That's why we firmly support The Travel Foundation, a charity that develops solutions to help improve and protect holiday destinations, their environment, traditions and culture. To find out what you can do to make a positive difference to the places you travel to and the people who live there, please visit *www.thetravelfoundation.org.uk*

Telephones

India has well-developed telecommunications. There are call booths, called STD-ISD PCOs (public call offices) on all the important highways and in towns, cities and villages that are usually cheaper than calling from hotels for national and international calls. Many PCOs have fax machines. Fax sending charges are based on phone rates with a supplement per page and the PCOs will receive facsimiles on your behalf

Ranked autorickshaws, Andhra Pradesh

for a per page fee. There are also coin-operated phones that are an inexpensive option for calling locally. Phone cards for cell phones called 'mobile cards' are available in India.

Time
Indian Standard Time is $5^1/_2$ hours ahead of GMT.

Toilets
Public toilets are rarely clean in India, and they are almost always of the 'hole in the ground' variety. When travelling, look for hotels and smart restaurants that are likely to have westernised cloakrooms. Keep soap and a stock of tissues handy, and, especially if travelling with children, carry a supply of antiseptic wet wipes.

Travellers with disabilities
Unfortunately, India has limited facilities for disabled visitors. Getting around in a wheelchair on Indian pavements is difficult, few hotels and monuments have ramps for wheelchair access, and bathrooms are rarely accessible for the physically challenged. Hiring a car for the tour is a possible solution as Indian drivers are usually extremely helpful.

Weights and measures
India uses the metric system, where distances are in kilometres and weights in grams and kilograms. However, some imperial methods of measurement are still used in places.

CONVERSION TABLE

FROM	TO	MULTIPLY BY
Inches	Centimetres	2.54
Feet	Metres	0.3048
Yards	Metres	0.9144
Miles	Kilometres	1.6090
Acres	Hectares	0.4047
Gallons	Litres	4.5460
Ounces	Grams	28.35
Pounds	Grams	453.6
Pounds	Kilograms	0.4536
Tons	Tonnes	1.0160

To convert back, for example from centimetres to inches, divide by the number in the third column.

MEN'S SUITS

UK	36	38	40	42	44	46	48
Rest of Europe	46	48	50	52	54	56	58
USA	36	38	40	42	44	46	48

DRESS SIZES

UK	8	10	12	14	16	18
France	36	38	40	42	44	46
Italy	38	40	42	44	46	48
Rest of Europe	34	36	38	40	42	44
USA	6	8	10	12	14	16

MEN'S SHIRTS

UK	14	14.5	15	15.5	16	16.5	17
Rest of Europe	36	37	38	39/40	41	42	43
USA	14	14.5	15	15.5	16	16.5	17

MEN'S SHOES

UK	7	7.5	8.5	9.5	10.5	11
Rest of Europe	41	42	43	44	45	46
USA	8	8.5	9.5	10.5	11.5	12

WOMEN'S SHOES

UK	4.5	5	5.5	6	6.5	7
Rest of Europe	38	38	39	39	40	41
USA	6	6.5	7	7.5	8	8.5

Index

Acknowledgements

Thomas Cook Publishing wishes to thank the following libraries and associations for their assistance in the preparation of this book.

All pictures by DAVID HENLEY/CPA MEDIA except:

CHAWEEWAN CHUCHUAY 40, 61, 63, 69, 70, 179
DREAMSTIME Shailesh Nanal 95
RAINER KRACK/CPA MEDIA 15, 33, 38, 41, 43, 47, 49, 56, 65, 71, 74, 173, 175, 181, 182
DINESH SHUKLA 72, 79, 80, 125, 127, 129, 141
VASILE SZAKACS 7, 23, 34, 37, 55, 67, 73, 75, 76, 81, 119, 149, 151, 155, 157, 159, 161, 162, 163, 168, 169, 186, 188
THOMAS COOK TOUR OPERATIONS LTD 51, 58
WORLD PICTURES/PHOTOSHOT 1, 113

For CAMBRIDGE PUBLISHING MANAGEMENT LTD:
Project editor: Diane Teillol
Typesetter: Paul Queripel
Proofreader: Jan McCann
Indexer: Marie Lorimer

SEND YOUR THOUGHTS TO
BOOKS@THOMASCOOK.COM

We're committed to providing the very best up-to-date information in our travel guides and constantly strive to make them as useful as they can be. You can help us to improve future editions by letting us have your feedback. If you've made a wonderful discovery on your travels that we don't already feature, if you'd like to inform us about recent changes to anything that we do include, or if you simply want to let us know your thoughts about this guidebook and how we can make it even better – we'd love to hear from you.

Send us ideas, discoveries and recommendations today and then look out for your valuable input in the next edition of this title.

Emails to the above address, or letters to Travellers Series Editor, Thomas Cook Publishing, PO Box 227, Unit 9, Coningsby Road, Peterborough PE3 8SB, UK.

Please don't forget to let us know which title your feedback refers to!